Journey to the Hidden Kingdoms

by
Jim Mackenzie

A Guide to the Children's Books of Newcastle, North Tyneside and Northumberland

Jacket illustration by William Stobbs for "Silver Everything and Many Mansions"
(OUP 1976), reprinted by permission of Oxford University Press.

Published by Powdene Publicity Ltd.,
Unit 17, St. Peter's Wharf, Newcastle upon Tyne NE6 1TZ

© Jim Mackenzie and Powdene Publicity Ltd.

Front and back cover illustration by Mike Gay

Printed by Pensord, Pontllanfraith, Wales.

British Library Cataloguing in Publication Data

Mackenzie, Jim
Journey to the
Hidden Kingdoms

ISBN No. 0-9544493-1-2

Contents

Journey to the Hidden Kingdoms

CHILDREN'S stories are like a form of magic. They can stay in your mind long after the first reading and yet, in later life, it is sometimes almost impossible to recall the title and the author of the book that once charmed you so much. In this book I set out to trace all the children's stories that have been written about Newcastle, North Tyneside and Northumberland. For those of you born and brought up in this region, I hope this collection of over 100 "finds" manages to put you in touch again with the elusive stories of your youth and then perhaps you can pass them on to the next generation. For those of you who are visitors to the region I hope you will find that this is both an unusual and rewarding way to appreciate the delights of the lands that lie between County Durham and the Scottish border.

The best story always involves a journey and so the titles have been arranged as the four stages of a voyage. You see, as well as the hidden kingdom of our childhood which we all have to leave behind, there are the other hidden kingdoms of Newcastle, North Tyneside and Northumberland to be explored. This book hopes to take you on a journey through both space and time, travelling round the region as well as back into its recent and more distant past. For a journey you need a map and so I have constructed four of them – one for each stage of the journey. Together with local guidebooks and leaflets supplied by Northumbria Tourist Board, they should allow you to experience the settings of some of the stories at first hand.

A detailed account of every book mentioned would be prohibitively long and so I adopted a few simple principles. The most important was that the harder a book was to obtain, the greater the need to supply you with the story and the flavour of the experience. To a large extent recently published books have been dealt with quickly, though I hope enough has been said to help parents decide whether they would like to buy them for their children. I also hope that full justice has been done to the winners of prestigious prizes for children's literature: Richard Armstrong, Robert Westall, Aidan Chambers, Winifred Finlay, and Winifred Cawley, who were all born in the north-east of England. Notable prize-winning outsiders who have written about this region include Rosemary Sutcliff and Philip Turner.

As mentioned above there are over 100 stories in this book. However, almost one third of them were written by Lorna Hill who was born in Durham and lived a large part of her life as a vicar's wife in Matfen. Everywhere you go in each of the four stages of the journey you will encounter her stories. Inevitably some of the details have had to be missed out, though I hope you will agree that time after time she supplies us with descriptions of the town and the countryside that enliven and enrich our journey.

Of course quite a few stories won't be pigeon-holed into one stage only. This is well-illustrated by the first section on Newcastle where the story often starts but then is completed out in the countryside. In order not to miss the descriptions and the incidents I have sometimes resorted to the device of splitting the stories into their relevant sections and putting a note to that effect so that the reader can skip to the appropriate page, join up the bits and see what happens.

So I wish you "good luck" on your journey. My own pilgrimage as a seeker-out of local stories will never really be over. Perhaps you will uncover one I haven't thought of – I already know more will be being written even as I type these pages and you take the first step on the way into the "Hidden Kingdoms".

Jim Mackenzie, September 2003.

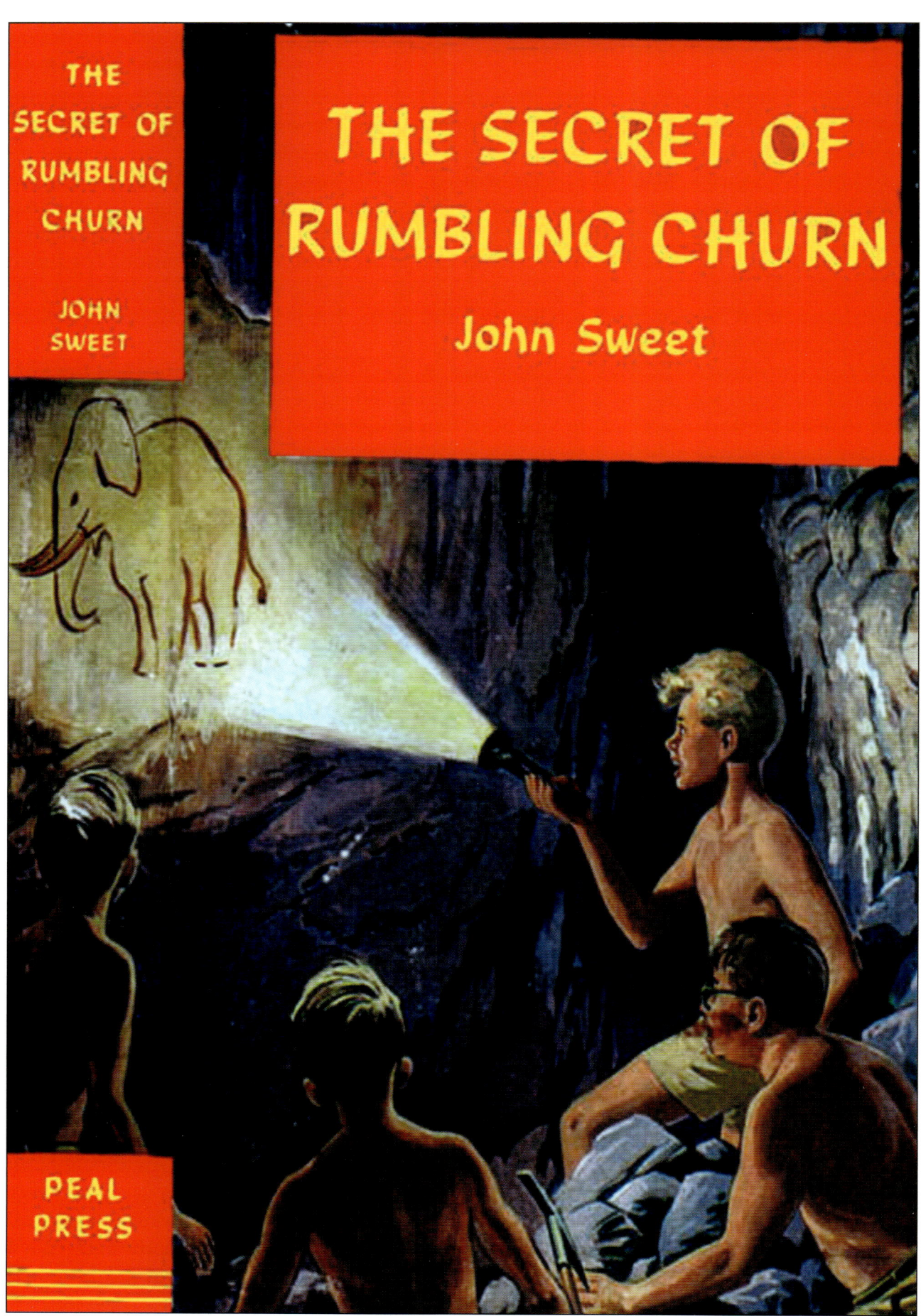

THE SECRET OF RUMBLING CHURN

JOHN SWEET

THE SECRET OF RUMBLING CHURN

John Sweet

PEAL PRESS

The Secret of Rumbling Churn – A Scout story set in deepest Northumberland.

On the left two "Patience" adventures and on the right two "Marjorie" adventures.

Acknowledgements

MUCH of the work for this book has been done in the Local Studies Department of the City Library of Newcastle upon Tyne, to whose staff I owe thanks for their assistance and patience.

Many of the books traced here were first mentioned by the members of two internet discussion groups. I should like to extend thanks to:

The Girlsown Group in general and Sally Dore and Betula O' Neill (booksellers par excellence) in particular.

The Collecting Books and Magazines Group in general with special mention of John Tipper, Barbara Cooper, Kim Miles (all of Australia) and David Anderson (of Vancouver, Canada).

Of course, my biggest debt of gratitude is owed to the authors and illustrators of the books that you will discover in the following pages. It has proved impossible so far to trace all copyright holders but my thanks are extended to the Children's Section at Oxford University Press for permission to use the dustjacket art of books by Winifred Cawley, Barbara Leonie Picard, Frederick Grice and Peter Carter and to Girls Gone By Publishing for some of the images from the work of Lorna Hill. I believe that my own journey to the "Hidden Kingdoms" began in a second-hand bookshop in Whitley Bay when I bought a copy of "Castle in Northumbria" by Lorna Hill. However, no sooner had I begun to read this adventure than other stories sprang from my memory demanding renewed attention.

Nevertheless, two authors claim my particular attention this year. The first is indeed Lorna Hill who wrote almost one third of the children's stories we can count as Northumbrian. Last year (2002) was the 100th anniversary of her birth in Durham. The second is Richard Armstrong, the son of a blacksmith from Walbottle, who went on to win the Carnegie Medal, and whose 100th anniversary fell on June 18th this year. The two authors and their stories couldn't be more different but they illustrate most clearly the variety and richness that lie waiting in the "Hidden Kingdoms".

Lorna Hill

Richard Armstrong

Index to the Availability of the Children's Stories in this guide

THE numbers in brackets refer to the order in which the stories appear and the way in which they are identified on the four maps; also given are page number references.

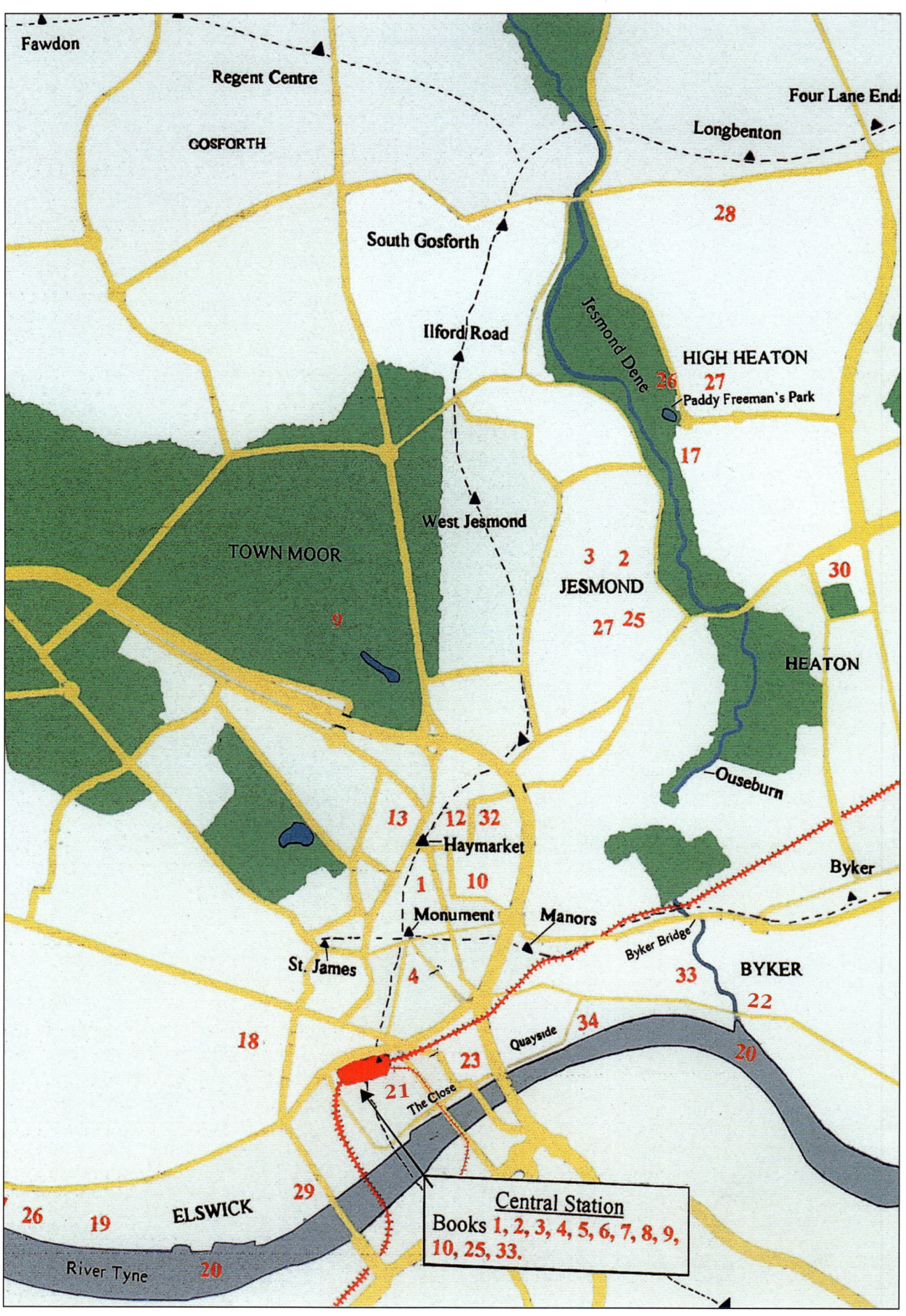

Fawdon

Regent Centre

GOSFORTH

Four Lane Ends

Longbenton

28

South Gosforth

Ilford Road

Jesmond Dene

HIGH HEATON

26 27

Paddy Freeman's Park

17

West Jesmond

TOWN MOOR

3 2

JESMOND

27 25

30

HEATON

9

—Ouseburn

Byker

13

12 32

—Haymarket

1 10

Monument

Manors

Byker Bridge

BYKER

33

St. James

4

22

18

Quayside 34

20

23

The Close

21

Central Station
Books 1, 2, 3, 4, 5, 6, 7, 8, 9,
10, 25, 33.

26 19 ELSWICK 29

River Tyne 20

8

Stage 1: Newcastle

BEFORE each stage of the journey you will find a map to indicate the area being discussed. The numbers on each map correspond with the books on the lists (see below) and with the numbers printed alongside the book title in the course of the account. Where an A,B or C is printed alongside the number in the account this means the book will have been split into different sections corresponding to the different locations. On rare occasions two books by the same author may be indicated by one number. Thus *Masquerade at the Wells* and *Jane Leaves the Wells* both tell the story of Jane and her cousin Mariella and their story is represented by the number 3. Similarly there is an overlap between the characters in Winifred Cawley's *Down the Long Stairs* and her sequel *Feast of the Serpent* and the numbers 21 and 22 have been used interchangeably for these two books.

   Where a book is numbered but does not appear on a map it indicates the location is too vague, e.g. "Newcastle in general", for trying to suggest the precise district in which the action happened.

 1. It was all through Patience – Lorna Hill (Central Station – Shops)
 2. A Dream of Sadler's Wells – Lorna Hill (Central Station – Jesmond)
 3. Jane Leaves the Wells – Lorna Hill (Central Station – Jesmond)
 4. The Hut on Oh Me Edge – L.E.O. Charlton (Central Station – Shops)
 5. Dark River, Dark Mountain – Sylvia Sherry (Central Station)
 6. Gran at Coalgate – Winifred Cawley (Central Station)
 7. Highland Twins at the Chalet School – Elinor M. Brent Dyer (Central Station)
 8. Wrong Gear – Margaret Storey (Central Station – Royal Victoria Infirmary)
 9. The Witch of Redesdale – Winifred Finlay (The Town Moor – Central Station)
10. Shadow Play – Terry Deary (Central Station – City Library – Groat Market)
11. Annerton Pit – Peter Dickinson (The City)
12. Storm Over Cheviot – Winifred Finlay (Haymarket)
13. Principal Role – Lorna Hill (Worswick Street – Haymarket)
14. Joe and the Magpie – Chris Mabbott (Quayside – St. James' Park – River Tyne – Jesmond Dene)
15. Tinseltoon – Christopher Goulding (Northumberland Street and shops)
16. Graingertoon – Christopher Goulding (Grainger Street and High Level Bridge)
17. Marle – Aidan Chambers (Jesmond Dene – Scotswood – Woolworth – Marks and Spencer)
18. More About Mandy – Lorna Hill (Rye Hill)
19. Sabotage at the Forge – Richard Armstrong (Elswick)
20. Heaven Eyes – David Almond (River Tyne – Ouse Burn)
21. Down the Long Stairs – Winifred Cawley (The Close – The Quayside – St. Nicholas)
22. Feast of the Serpent – Winifred Cawley (The Close – The Quayside – Ouse Burn)
23. Ransom for a Knight – Barbara Leonie Picard (The Close – The Quayside)
24. Danger at Black Dyke – Winifred Finlay (The City)
25. The Little Dancer – Lorna Hill (Jesmond – Central Station – Police Station)
26. Swan Feather – Lorna Hill (Elswick/Benwell – Jesmond Dene – Paddy Freeman's Park)
27. Mystery in the Middle Marches – Winifred Finlay (Jesmond – Paddy Freeman's Park
28. Rosanna Joins the Wells – Lorna Hill (Theatre Royal – High Heaton – Jesmond)
29. Dress Rehearsal – Lorna Hill (Tyne Bridges – West End)
30. Skellig – David Almond (Heaton)
31. Dunkirk Summer – Philip Turner (St. Ann's?)
32. Northern Lights – Lorna Hill (Grainger Street – Fenwick's – Haymarket)
33. The Secret – Lorna Hill (Byker Bridge, Ouseburn, Central Station, Jesmond)
34. Greenhorn – Richard Armstrong (Quayside)

The Threshold of Adventure

SO let us step off the train and start the journey. What better place to be introduced to the region than by passing through one of its more remarkable public buildings – John Dobson's masterpiece – Newcastle Central Station ? It is also fitting that we should begin this exploration of the region through the eyes of its most prolific writer of children's stories, Lorna Hill. Over 33 stories in all give us a very full picture of the city of Newcastle itself in its very different moods. Later her books will also take us out to see a particular way of life in the Tyne Valley and then amongst the more affluent members of society in wildest Northumberland.

It was all through Patience – 1952 (1) gives a perfect example of how Lorna Hill is able to use the settings of her books to establish and develop relationships. It begins on Central Station with the arrival of David from London and the different greetings that are given by the delighted and devoted Patience, the self-confident Richard and Elizabeth and the admiring but shy Judy. A quick sketch of the sounds and sights of the noisy station is followed by Lorna Hill's description of a 1950s Newcastle that is by contrast quiet, peaceful and, in a way, beautiful. It is a city of trolley-buses that scurry like beetles, cars with headlights resembling fireflies and traffic lights like "exotic, jewelled flowers". Yet each of the children knows that the city is only showing this attractive face to them because of their joy at being together again. Other, less pleasant occasions, when the town appeared a gloomy enemy, are recalled and serve to make this reunion all the brighter by contrast.

More real landmarks and familiar Newcastle places are then placed before us as the children make their way through the city as evening falls. There is Tilley's restaurant where Elizabeth drools over the cakes in the window and they make their way over the thick carpet to eat their tea-time treats. David's generous and friendly nature is established by the sacrifice of his pocket money so that all his friends are happy. Later, however, Judy succumbs to the temptation of being the model for a make-up demonstration in a department store (Fenwick's) and finds herself the object of his scorn and his anger. There then follows an eerie description of a visit to the top floor cloakroom (in an attempt to wash off the offending cosmetics) and then coming downstairs through a succession of closed up departments as the store shuts for the night. Lorna Hill captures perfectly that strange feeling of suddenly seeing something familiar from an unexpected and slightly disturbing perspective. Later Judy's punishment for trying the lipstick and the make-up is to be deceived into thinking that it won't come off for months – Jungle Night lips no longer seem so attractive.

Now the children are ready for their trip out to their homes in Northumberland and the prospect of holiday adventures up on the wild moors.

The station and Newcastle itself, you see, have merely been the threshold to adventure. Let us return to the station and start again. For it is really quite astonishing how many times it acts as the prelude to the narrative.

Lorna Hill's stories were mostly written as parts of long series, the most well-known of which is the "Sadler's Wells" sequence based around the world of ballet. To fulfil their destiny as ballet dancers the young heroines have to leave their homes in the north and travel to London. Throughout the long saga of fourteen books there is much coming and going via the rail link to the south and there are many memorable scenes both on the trains and on the platforms. Indeed the very first of the books, ***A Dream of Sadler's Wells*** – 1950 (2) has the overall series heroine, fourteen year old Veronica Weston, meeting the eccentric but talented hero, Sebastian Scott, on the train from London. As you might expect their touchy and stormy friendship eventually turns into something more profound. Arrivals and departures are always charged with emotion and Lorna Hill makes full use of the possibilities presented. Veronica herself undergoes a wild overnight cross-country dash at the end of this first book, arriving at Central Station at four o'clock in the morning to catch the train to London to get to a vital audition that may be her "big chance". The train leaves at six o'clock and she and Sebastian put their heads down and doze at a table in the waiting room until roused by the woman in charge who has been handsomely tipped to ensure they wake up. On this occasion Veronica heads south, clutching a hired rug to keep her warm during the long journey. However, as each heroine, whether it be Veronica, Jane, Ella, Rosanna, Sylvia, Nona or Vanessa, climbs the ladder of success, their travelling arrangements become increasingly more luxurious with details of "sleepers" and private compartments. The girls arrive in London or Newcastle having woken from slumber with all the facilities that British Railways could provide. This doesn't necessarily diminish the tension of each greeting or departure on the platform. One of the best scenes comes in *Jane Leaves the Wells* – 1953 (3A – see page 58 for 3B) where the original timid little girl of the first part of her story has become transformed in confidence by her time away from home and her ballet training. Brought up in a pony-riding and hunting household, she is now prepared to state her own very different views and, standing on the platform amidst her suitcases, makes her point defiantly about the cruelty involved in creating fur coats (A subject about which Lorna Hill herself was passionate).

Arrivals and Departures

However, it is time to chronicle a few more of the literary arrivals and departures from this well-known landmark. The same refreshment and waiting room where Veronica dozed is the scene for one of those classic "overhearing" ploys that so often form the kernel of a mystery plot. In *The Hut on Oh Me Edge* – 1949 (4A – see page 87 for 4B) by Air Commodore L.E.O. Charlton, cousins Frank and John are bemoaning their lot for their school at Otterburn has been closed because of a polio outbreak and they haven't sufficient funds to go camping on the Northumberland moors. As they dally over the "coarse and unattractive food" served by the refreshment room, the stranger who had been doing the eavesdropping sympathises with their predicament and offers them a job. All they have to do is to live in a hut on Oh Me Edge and write a diary of all that happens. As we shall see, the wilds of Northumberland are classic L.E.O. Charlton territory, but, before Frank and John get to their hut they have to travel back to Newcastle from their closed-up home in Yorkshire. They pause to buy themselves a map at a "double-windowed" stationers in the city centre (probably the Mawson Swann and Morgan building that has now become Waterstones) and find themselves under suspicion of passing forged money. We later find that the gang had its headquarters in Jesmond! Eventually Frank and John satisfy the authorities and set off for the hills on their trusty motorbike called Emma. We will join them later.

Before we look at few more incomers, it is time to devote a minute to those from this region who pass through the station on their way to adventures in territories that are beyond the brief of this book. Sylvia Sherry's *Dark River, Dark Mountain* – 1975 (5) concerns the evacuation of a wartime refugee and his adventures in the Pennines, the consequences of which come back to haunt him many years later when he suddenly reads an article as he sits on the top tier of a Newcastle bus. As the train pulls out of the station the author gives us all too brief a glimpse of the back streets as the young man goes off to meet his fate. A much younger child is Winifred Cawley's Jinnie Friend who, exhausted by the strain of the impending 11 plus scholarship examination, sets off from her home in Wallsend to take a short holiday with her Grandmother in County Durham. In *Gran at Coalgate* – 1974 (6) Jinnie is entrusted to the railway authorities before the train chugs off south over the Tyne via the famous diamond crossing and the High Level Bridge. The track to Leadgate near Consett is long gone and the rest of the story must be told elsewhere, for we have more arrivals to greet before we can finally leave the station.

Central Station – A train snakes over the famous diamond crossing.

The biggest of the "Big Four" writers of school stories for girls is Elinor M. Brent-Dyer who was born in South Shields. In spite of this northern association, the mentions of her native territory are very few and far between in her long 59 book "Chalet School" series. The most extended reference comes in **Highland Twins at the Chalet School** – 1942 (7) where the girls in question travel across Northumberland and Tyneside at the height of the Second World War. There is a rapidly sketched portrait of Newcastle Central Station, which proves so noisy and full of people that there is some difficulty about catching the train on to Leeds. A similar brief vision of the station is presented in the story of troubled runaway teenager Maggie in Margaret Storey's **Wrong Gear** – 1973 (8), who has been involved in a car crash in County Durham and who has just visited the Royal Victoria Infirmary to see the injured driver. The train south will take her back to face life in London with her father and her new step-mother.

Most of the time there is something rather alluring about young people arriving at Central Station and setting off through Newcastle for adventures in Northumberland. This is captured most effectively by Winifred Finlay's first book, **The Witch of Redesdale** – 1951 (9A – see page 90 for 9B). Take, for instance, the idea of two boys and two girls in their mid-teenage years (and not from the same family) going away on a cycling holiday together without their parents so much as turning a hair about what might happen, or establishing what the exact feelings were between the persons involved. The gentle repartee of boy-girl friendship without sexual overtones has a charm of its own that Winifred Finlay brings out effortlessly as the adventure unfolds amongst the rugged Northumberland countryside. From the start familiar places and stories greet the reader everywhere. There is the bedlam of the girls' arrival at Newcastle Central Station followed by the careful journey up Grey Street and Northumberland Street and then out alongside the Town Moor. Later, as they follow the Newcastle to Jedburgh road to the Catcleugh Reservoir, the details of the Border Ballads are related to the hills and heather that surround them by the romantic Gill who has learned so many lines of poetry by heart. What could be better ?

A *Murder Mystery*

And now we must have a contrast. Not everyone arriving by train in Newcastle faces such a happy and relatively innocent world.

Sex, violence and murder are three topics that you might not expect to find in a book which was written for children. However, the story **Shadow Play** – 1992 (10) by Terry Deary was clearly intended for older teenagers and none of the details included in the story-line is either graphic or offensive, though the topics dealt with are compellingly adult.

The first thing to make clear is that the story is meticulously plotted and moves at a relentless pace. It would be unfair in a review of a book which is basically a "whodunnit" to give away too many of the twists and turns. Always remember that there are two possible pleasures to be gained by reading this sort of book. If the author succeeds in baffling you until the end, then you have the satisfaction of the surprise revelations. However, if you guess who is guilty before you are told, then you have almost a greater satisfaction in knowing that you were right – that in some way you were smarter than the author.

There are two stories in this book and, as the title hints, one is a shadow outline of the other. Both stories are murder stories. One is set in Newcastle in the present time and the other is set in County Durham in the past. One has sprung from the imagination of Terry Deary, the other is the all-too-real case of Mary Ann Cotton, the mass murderer who was hanged for her crimes. The investigations of Arthur Appleton, a real north-east journalist, into the infamous deeds of the most notorious woman in the region was the acknowledged source for what is described in "Shadow Play". Deary even introduces the "Arthur" figure as a journalist in his story and then callously "bumps him off" as he drives the events towards the climax. However, an affectionate tribute to "Arthur" by the honest policeman makes it clear that this author knows the debt he owes to the original research.

While Arthur Appleton knew all there was to know about the famous poisoner, it soon becomes clear that Terry Deary knows all about the experience of theatre in schools. Small theatre groups, sometimes employed by the council, sometimes by the school itself, travel round the educational establishments in the area, and perform improvised plays with the minimum of actors, props and scenery. Nowadays sheer necessity and pressure of time force the plays to be mostly important scenes from set texts studied for GCSE or National Curriculum Tests. However, there is also a tradition of taking local themes and stories and making them come alive. The actors in these plays are often young men and women at the beginning of their stage careers, learning the ropes of the business and scarcely more than two or three years older than their audiences.

Graham Gooden, the first-person narrator of this story, has been accepted by such a group and has arrived at Newcastle Central Station on a foggy evening to take up his post. His lodgings are in Hope Street and, when he finally arrives there, he hears a scream in the darkness as he draws near to number 39. Little does he know that his nightmare has begun. After a restless night's sleep in his upstairs room he comes down to find that the dead body of the fifteen year old landlady's daughter has been found on the ground outside. Is it accident, suicide or murder ? Pretty soon it becomes clear that murder is most likely and Graham realises that the occupants of the house and their associates are the main suspects. The other three members of the group: Helen Trayne, Peter France and Anna Morriso are also lodgers and the director of the group is a friend of the landlady. As the story proceeds each of them, including Graham, comes under suspicion. The dead girl was pregnant and a "who is the father ? " investigation continues alongside the homicide case.

Meanwhile, for the theatre group, life must go on. They have been commissioned to produce something about famous north-east women. The director sends them away in pairs to research so that they can return and improvise scenes on what they have found. Peter and Anna decide to look at the life of Bessie Surtees; Helen and Graham decide to find out about Mary Ann Cotton. The place they go to is the City Library, Newcastle, which, as you might expect, is the main scene for the researches in the book you are now reading.

From this point onwards the two cases begin indeed to "shadow" each other. By trying to get under the skin of Mary Ann Cotton and discover what made such an attractive woman commit so many murders, they find that they are addressing some of the same issues that are involved in the case of the dead girl at their lodgings. (Incidentally the Bessie Surtees story is dismissed as too boring.) In the case of both Mary Ann Cotton and the recently-murdered Debbie the problem of sexual attraction is a part of the motivation and the disposal of unwanted babies certainly comes into consideration. The dead fifteen year old was almost certainly promiscuous and there are references to the men she flirted with in pubs in what Deary calls "Groat Street". Mary Ann Cotton had a series of husbands and lovers and children by different men. Each of these characters becomes a witness in a mock trial that the young actors and their director stage as a part of their rehearsal. As one of them is a possible murderer each line that is said is often barbed with a double meaning. The author then stirs in the inevitable sexual attractions between young actors at the height of their powers which further complicates the feelings that are let loose.

The second murder is that of Arthur, the reporter who believed he had discovered the key to what had motivated Mary Ann Cotton's extraordinary crimes. The third murder attempted is on the storyteller himself...

More details would give away too much. The guilty person can be identified by a close observation of the clues, but the driving pace of the action means that you have to be very quick-thinking to spot it. That is one challenge of this book. The second problem that the author sets you is a deeper one. He wants you to explore with him the world of Mary Ann Cotton, one of the most hideous women ever to live in this region. Can we possibly enter this "lost domain" of evil that existed in the mind of the murderess from County Durham and come away with some understanding and compassion ?

Motorbikes, Buses and Cars

But there are more ways of arriving in Newcastle than by the train.

A unique evocation of Newcastle and the countryside of Northumberland is provided in the extraordinary story of **Annerton Pit** – 1977 (11A – see page 43 for 11B) by Peter Dickinson. It is unique because the narrative is mostly constructed from the point of view of the central character, Jake, who has been blind from birth. All his impressions, and thus all our impressions, are ways of "seeing" through the other senses. This makes us think twice about what lies behind the superficial surface of the environment that surrounds us. The reader is forced to come to the region again as a different kind of stranger.

Jake and his elder brother, Martin, come north from Southampton in search of their grandfather who has failed to send his usual Braille postcard for several weeks. Their own clues to his whereabouts lie in their knowledge of his usual habits and procedures. The old man's hobby, which he has been free to pursue since his retirement, is the investigation and debunking of local haunted places and the associated superstitions. To find his trail they will have to visit the library of the local newspaper where he will have traced local legends and contacted people with local knowledge.

Before that, however, we are given Jake's reactions as, perched on the pillion seat of the BMW motorbike behind Martin, he draws nearer to Newcastle. At first the results of his "seeing" procedure appear disappointingly naïve. For him the air has become smokier and the buildings have suddenly become taller. Later, as he lies in the room in the church hostel, he becomes aware of the wind-borne smell of the sea. One is forced to wonder if this is the over-fanciful imagination of the writer or a sensation that is really there but blanketed for us today by our overwhelming sense of sight.

However, there are other "seeing" observations by Jake that are more immediately convincing. As they follow in the footsteps of their grandfather, the young boy finds himself noticing details of the north-east accent, in particular the way in which some people affect a more refined mode of speech but are constantly betrayed by their flattened vowels. Others seem to form every sentence they utter as if they were framing a string of questions. Each new person the readers are introduced to is identified by the nuances of his voice and the sounds of his movement. After a time, having established this curious authenticity about Jake's methods for reading personality, mood and character, Peter Dickinson shifts the focus of the blind boy's mental radar on to the nature of the countryside. And so we move outside the city again.

If Winifred Finlay's characters set off for distant Northumberland on bikes in *The Witch of Redesdale* she varies her approach in **Storm Over Cheviot** – 1955 (12A – see page 91 for 12B). The story begins in the Haymarket bus station, Newcastle, and ends in a remote house in the upper College Valley. It reflects on the friendships and rivalries between boys and girls and then narrows its focus to the fortunes of one particular adult.

When you miss the bus it must seem like good fortune is smiling on you if the driver of a top-class Jaguar offers you a lift to the very place that you are going. Richard and Paul Norton and their uncle Bill Wright are starting a winter walking holiday at Carter Bar. Young Richard lives in an imaginary world of his own, re-fighting the border battles as Sir Richard Norton, the scourge of the Scots. Thus when Flash Baker invites the three of them into his car and sets off north he listens intently to the young man's stories of his smart-alec attitude to life. It is clear that Flash spends much of his time living on the margins between what is morally reprehensible and what is actually illegal. Both Bill and Paul are glad when their lift is at an end and they can set off for their trek across the empty border countryside.

The Haymarket features again in **Principal Role** – 1957 (13) by Lorna Hill. This time it is that well-known literary invention "Ruritania", the mythical European country, which in the person of Princess Fazia of Slavonia has come north to Newcastle. She arrives by bus from Durham at what must be the old Worswick Street bus station and finds that she has to transfer to the Haymarket in order to catch the bus to Blackheath (a thinly-disguised Consett).

"The Princess followed her directions and walked obediently up a long straight street lined with shops, all prettily decorated for Christmas. Crowds of shoppers were pouring in and out of them. Above the largest was an outsize figure of Santa Claus and his sleigh, outlined with twinkling lights and banked by holly and evergreens. At the top of the street was a wide square with a church in the middle of it. At its door stood a tall Christmas tree on whose branches winked and twinkled hundreds of fairy-lights. It was very pretty, but the Princess hardly saw it – she was so cold and hungry !"

Things get much worse for Fazia some time later when after her next bus journey, nearly frozen to death, she tumbles into a ditch exhausted. But that's in County Durham and out of our territory again.

Newcastle – old and new, ugly and beautiful

The Picture Books

So far we have simply passed through the city en route to a larger world outside, but what have children's authors got to say about the place itself ? The simplest vision comes, naturally enough, in basic children's picture books.

Chris Mabbott was responsible for the illustrations on **Joe and the Magpie** – 2000 (14) and shares the credit for the research and writing of the story-line with Christine Revel.

This little book is an attempt to answer the question "Is Newcastle boring ?" with a resounding "No !" Joe, resting in a sleepy state by the side of the Ouse Burn in Jesmond Dene, is bored with life in general and with Newcastle in particular. His reverie is interrupted by a magpie which is gifted in at least three different ways, and who dearly wants Joe to appreciate all that lies around him. The first gift is that of speech, and part of the charm of the book is the lively, almost impudent attitude shown by the bird as it guides Joe and us through the rest of the story.

The second and third gifts that the bird possesses are the capacities to move both in space and in time. To his surprise Joe finds himself whisked out over the River Tyne and put into contact with the crew of one of the old keel boats. In quick succession there follow scenes down by the quayside where Joe befriends some youngsters from an earlier and much harsher era. The banter between the boys from the different centuries is used to show how lads are much the same at any time, but the conditions they face are very different. Modern Joe wants a burger but has to make do with an old-fashioned pie.

Later scenes recall important events in Newcastle's colourful history, including disasters such as the terrible plague epidemic of 1853 and the cataclysmic great fire, and small triumphs such as the forming of Newcastle United from the different minor clubs. There are scenes at St. James' Park and an adventure on the Swing Bridge, whilst all the time the magpie is both recounting the history, answering Joe's questions, and occasionally displaying unusual and very human traits in his character. He doesn't like to talk, for example, of the stuffed magpie which is the unofficial mascot of the great football team.

The familiar "Was it all a dream ?" plot construction technique brings the story to an end with Joe back by the waterfall and wondering whether the memento in his pocket proves that it really did happen. Though a little random in its selection of the history it covers, the book engages and holds the attention well with its lively drawings and its cheeky and irreverent narrator.

Christopher Goulding has written two books illustrated by Chris Mabbott, in which the centre of Newcastle is brought to life in a very unusual way. *Tinseltoon* – 1998 (15) records the events on one Christmas Eve when all the statues of Newcastle gradually come to life. From Harry Hotspur to George Stephenson and from Jackie Milburn with his football to the rabbit behind the cathedral, all begin to take advantage of the magic dust sprinkled on them by the fairy from the top of the Northern Goldsmiths' clock. Grainger the cat is the surprised witness to this outbreak of celebration which soon gets delightfully out of hand. Local landmarks all feature in this lively illustrated adventure which has scenes down by the River Tyne and in front of Fenwick's Christmas window display. *Graingertoon* – 1999 (16) is the sequel to this first adventure and this time the young cat learns some of the history of the town from his grandma. The highlight is when a plague of rats is successfully driven into the river by an animated version of the High Level Bridge which stalks the streets of Newcastle in a satisfyingly menacing fashion.

When we move from picture books to prose stories we begin to find that Newcastle is a place which conjures up many different images. We have already seen how so many people pass through on their way to the greatly different coast and countryside scenes that lie out in rural Northumberland. We can now use this contrast to explore more closely the nature of the city itself. So let's move out into a very special place in order to take a clear look back.

From Inside and Outside

The author calls the island *Marle* – (17) but in Aidan Chambers' book of the same name published in 1968, all the important details correlate with the well-known features of Holy Island. When the action moves for a while to the city the author makes no secret of the fact that it is Newcastle that he is describing. The essence of the book is the contrast of the two environments and the conflicting pulls they exert upon the central character, Kevin. For most of the action of the book Kevin is confused, trying to make sense of what he actually wants from the world. The interplay of people and places and the doubts and worries of a seventeen year old are all neatly worked out by an author who clearly has a feel for the differing environments, even if his descriptions of actual places are not developed in detail.

Susan and Kevin are the only seventeen year olds on the island. Though they find enjoyment in each other's company, there has never been any declaration of affection between them. It is only when Susan has gone to Newcastle that Kevin realises that life on the island is becoming intolerable. The author skilfully gives an impression of a community that is contracting and dying. The prospects for Kevin look remarkably bleak. Susan has gone to seek a new life, Kevin's grandfather is eking out an existence as a master boatbuilder who hardly has any work to do on the boats that are left, and Kevin's father spends too much time in the local pub and seems bereft of any purpose in life apart from challenging his son's ideas. When the letters from Susan stop coming Kevin knows that the time has come for him to make a change. He too decides to move to Newcastle.

The impressions that we are given of the city are more reflective of Kevin's mood than of any opinions that should be regarded as permanent. As a boy used to the quiet rhythm of the country, he is overwhelmed by the baffling pace and the "set" and "glum" faces of the pedestrians he encounters. Every one seems locked into their own little world, without any consideration for others. Yet at night time the streets seem to bring an air of jauntiness and good humour that they lacked during the day. Susan's job at the Woolworths' shop seems remarkably mundane but she has found a boyfriend called Chris who makes her evenings carefree and enjoyable. There may be a place for Kevin in this new world but, it would seem, not alongside Susan whom he now feels that he loves. Meantime Kevin lives in an anonymous suburb with his aunt and uncle and works at a small dinghy construction business based in Scotswood. At times the city can still feel cold and lonely but he begins to find the people friendly, even Chris, the older lad who has taken Susan away from him. He settles in to working hard and trying to think of ways of winning Susan back.

The sudden serious illness of his grandfather takes him back to the island. Before the old man dies he tells Kevin that he is to inherit the boat-building business. The crisis of the book has been reached. The city and the possibility of winning back Susan exert their influence in one direction. The pull of home and trying to make something of his inheritance are in direct contradiction. He returns to Newcastle to talk to Susan and make his decision. Fortunately it is her half-day off work and the two go to Jesmond Dene and sit talking together by the side of a small waterfall. Later they take a trip out to the airport.

The sudden opportunity to go for a short flight brings all Kevin's thoughts to the point where he can make a decision. The pilot has taken them on a short journey up the coast and Kevin sees the island from a different perspective. The familiarity has hidden the potential that he now realises for the first time. Excitedly he pours out his new ideas to Susan. Whether they will work or not doesn't matter: he has now gained the purpose in life that makes all the difference to him.

The end of the book is a postscript in the form of a letter from Kevin to Susan who still lives in Newcastle three years later. He has adapted his grandfather's business so that they now build sailing boats and this has helped in the development of tourism. Business on the island is now gradually looking up. Kevin has become a man by taking on the challenge of something near to home. He has learned how to discuss and negotiate and to push forward with his plans in spite of difficulties. Meanwhile Susan has merely progressed from Woolworths to Marks and Spencers, still serving in the coffee shop. Susan too had experienced a new view of "Marle" when on the flight three years before. She is now returning home, though whether the return is temporary or permanent is left open. Her boyfriend, Chris, is not mentioned but any possibility of a relationship with Kevin is uncertain. The island is no longer a "hole" that she had to get out of and Kevin is no longer a boy, unsure of himself. The reader is allowed to wonder whether what was once between them when they were seventeen can ever be rekindled.

Perhaps it is a story that could have been set anywhere. As it is told in the first person the reader is meant to get closer to Kevin who is in the process of "finding himself". Is it the place you live, the people you love or the job that you do which should matter most in your life ? Is it essential to move away before you can see the virtues and potential of the place that you have left behind ? Is the quality of life better in a small community or in a big city ? These are the questions that face any young person, and the polarised locations of the quietness of Holy Island and the bustle of the city of Newcastle are ideally suited as backdrops against which to explore them.

West End, Quayside, and River

A more clear-cut condemnation of life in the city comes in **More About Mandy** – 1963 (18) by Lorna Hill. After her early years spent in a rural Northumberland vicarage, seventeen year old Allison's attempts to break away to independence by taking up a job and a flat in Newcastle are marred by her lack of common sense and her poor judgement of character. Again the reader is given a very unattractive picture of life in a flat in the west end of Newcastle (somewhere like Rye Hill) and of the morals of Allison's "city slicker" friend who is prepared to use deception and theft in order to further her life-style. The values of the countryside are shown to be deeper and more secure. Allison's younger sister, Mandy, has a common sense and modesty that throws her sister's foolishness and selfishness into sharp contrast.

Let's look at a more positive picture. If we take a left turn from Central Station and walk down Forth Banks until we reach the River Tyne and walk then upstream, we would eventually reach the place that used to be Armstrong's famous factory: "gannin along the Scotswood Road" as the "Blaydon Races" would have it. And here we reach the story that immortalises the vision of Newcastle which perhaps still dominates the minds from outside the region. Most of the character of this area has been swept away by urban renewal and, though the riverside walk is pleasant, this "lost world" is better seen in the old pictures and in the writings of Richard Armstrong. For **Sabotage at the Forge** – 1946 (19) has the unusual setting of a Tyneside steelworks. Thias Stringer, a boy of fifteen, has worked as a greaser on the two thousand ton metal press for over a year. During the course of the book both he and the reader are to learn many details of this job and the various others that are essential to smooth running of the huge factory. However, a good children's story needs both conflict and a mystery if it is to support both evocative descriptions of places and careful explanations of the characters and skills of the men.

From the start of the first chapter the author makes it clear that there is something very wrong in the world of Thias and his fellow apprentices. The problem is bullying. Bull Chadwick, a furnaceman in the forge, has no time for boys. He spends his life devising ways of plaguing their lives with mean little tricks that bring hours of discomfort and misery for the boys, who cannot fight back against the strongest man in the works. An episode in which Bull humiliates a one-handed messenger boy from the clerk's office puts the reader firmly on the side of the spirited Thias as he tries to organise first of all defiance and then vengeance on the man who is the bane of all their lives.

Yet Richard Armstrong allows us to pass no easy verdict on this seemingly detestable man. He makes it clear that Bull is a workman who possesses tremendous skill and strength and he is well respected by all the other men in the factory. Outside the workplace he is liked for he is always the first to volunteer to use his strength to help people to shift heavy furniture, or to dig hard and stony gardens. The boys themselves can't understand why he dislikes them so much and takes such trouble to be vindictive towards them. They can only take refuge in the vague idea that he just happens to be "that way".

Thias' attempts to hit back at the bully, and the insight he thus gains into the way in which he can motivate the other apprentices brings out in a remarkably astute way all the frustrations that people face when they first try to assert leadership. However, Armstrong very cleverly leaves the problems with Bull simmering at the back of Thias' mind by starting two new lines of plot development. The young greaser is transferred to a different part of the factory and takes on a more responsible job. A new contract for gun-tubes also means a challenging change in working practices and very soon things start to go wrong. A thoroughly alarmed Thias begins to find clues which lead him to think that someone is engaged in sabotage. There is also the worrying mystery of what has happened to the master forgeman, old Jackie Rigden, who has just been retired after sixty to seventy years of skilled work and who has totally disappeared. The working out of each situation and the untangling of what actually happened are developed with the smoothness of a master craftsman. This is a story that you need to follow through to the very end.

More than that, however, the descriptions of the heat, the noise, the dull routine and the excitement of the work in a large factory are a worthy tribute to the industries that made the Tyneside region renowned throughout the world for metal products that were ingenious, strong and reliable. Armstrong's own experiences before he went to sea were in just such a factory and at times the words flow onto the page with a lyrical intensity. Yet the grim squalor of the spoil dump and the ravaged banks of the once beautiful river are also a part of the story. Just as old Jackie struggles to convey to young Thias the almost magical quality of steel and the sweat and the strength and the skill that makes it live, so Armstrong tries to leave for his readers an indelible memory of just what it was like to be a workman in such a place. In his account of how the factory grew he conjures up the past, and, in the explanation of how they adapt to the new development of the special gun-tube, he shows managers and men facing the challenges of the future. In the end we realise that "Sabotage at the Forge" as well as being an engrossing story of a boy coping with a job and finding his route to maturity, is also a valuable and memorable record of the region's industrial heritage.

A very different sort of story, a story that verges on the edge of fantasy, now takes us out on to the River Tyne itself. David Almond has stated that he believes that children want to explore the unknown and yet know that home is safely nearby. He follows this idea in *Heaven Eyes* – 2000 (20) where he takes his set of children on a journey of discovery down the Tyne. Take the word "home". The characters in *Heaven Eyes* are children without a true home – in old fashioned parlance they are orphans or foundlings. Erin's mother has died and January's mother has abandoned him. It was inevitable that they would be placed in a "home", which, at first sight because of the seeming institutionalised rituals and rather clumsy counselling, appears to be a violation of all that a home should be. And yet, for some of the inmates of Whitegates (probably on the opposite side of the river to Armstrong's factory), home is their shared destiny and the affinity that even the most "damaged" of them can feel for each other. It becomes the place that they have to go back to and, in the case of January, it's the place where home will come to him and he can leave. His arrival is a departure and his departure is an arrival. This same possibility of contradictory concepts contained within the one word occurs constantly throughout the book and gives it an intensified poetic quality. It is clear, for instance, that Erin's mother is both "dead" and yet "alive" and that Heaven Eyes both is and isn't her sister.

The voyage itself is both a long and a short one. The places mentioned are both real and they are not. Although he uses the word "Norton" for the city on a few occasions it is clear that he was thinking of Newcastle, and there are references to both the Tyne Bridge in its actuality and its representation in old photographs as the steel girders

Old mills and warehouses by the side of the Ouse Burn. The one in the background is soon to be "The Centre for the Children's Book".

arched towards each other. The Black Middens mentioned in this story are not the Black Middens near the mouth of the Tyne which so preoccupy the characters in Robert Westall's *The Watch House*. Is the Ouse Burn which flows into the river from the north the one that David Almond wants us to think about when he mentions the children washing themselves clean of the Black Middens mud ? It's just the right distance for the sounds of the city to travel. However, as with "Helmouth" in Almond's *Secret Heart*, there is just enough information to suggest real places and just enough vagueness for a child's imagination to supply the details and make it his or her own world that the author has guided him to. At the end of *Heaven Eyes* there are enough bits of paper and photographs for the Anna who is Heaven Eyes to emerge from the fantasy world that has sustained her for so long since the tragedy to her family. However, one of the messages of the book is clearly to let the realities of the world come naturally and allow the children the freedom to live in their imaginations.

An ironic but not unpleasant footnote can now be added to this account of an author who is now recognised as being at the forefront of writing for children in this region. Many of the old warehouses and factories along the Quayside and at the mouth of the Ouse Burn are now derelict and ripe for redevelopment. The heavy steel ball that will smash away the brickwork and the signs of ancient industry and trade invoked by David Almond in *Heaven Eyes* has already made its presence felt. New housing developments and leisure facilities stretch out from Newcastle down the river towards the sea. Some of the territory of *Heaven Eyes* has gone for ever. Yet, up the little Ouse Burn, an old warehouse lies in wait, ready for conversion. The Centre for the Children's Book is intended to provide not just a storage reservoir of books from the world of children's literature but a place where there will be an opportunity for authors and children to exchange ideas and experiences. It all serves to confirm Erin's prophetic words.

"The most extraordinary things existed in our ordinary world and just waited for us to find them."

Back into the Distant Past

When we return from our riverside walk or from Scotswood Road and walk back to the area beneath the High Level Bridge, it takes us down to the Close and the oldest surviving part of the city. It also allows us to travel back into the remarkable vision of Newcastle in two books by Winifred Cawley.

The first of these books is ***Down the Long Stairs*** – 1964 (21A – see page 35 for 21B). Fourteen year old Ralph Cole was born in Newcastle on the day that the ill-fated King Charles I passed through on his way to Scotland. Ralph is the son of a rich hostman, one of the guild of merchants who had exclusive rights over the trading of coal from the banks of the Tyne. As he tells the reader in his own first-person account, his journey towards maturity first began on the day he rebelled against the remarriage of his mother. It is bad enough that his father died fighting unsuccessfully against the Roundheads for King Charles, but now his mother is preoccupied with holding onto the family business and is lowering herself by marriage to one whom Ralph regards as little more than a servant. In a country and a city torn apart by those who are for Parliament and those who are for the King, young Ralph little realises that his hot-headedness will ensure that his own family will be placed in extreme jeopardy. Without thinking, he makes a decision which will alter the course of his life forever.

Winifred Cawley quickly conveys a picture of the spoiled child, living at the heart of Newcastle at a house in the Close, near the Quayside. Though his mother's time is taken up with the coal trade, Ralph basks in the affection of his old nurse, Alyse, and his young sister, Emmet. The days are marked by the comfortable chiming of the hours by the clock in St. Nicholas' Church.

To get to this world today you can walk along from Central Station to the Castle or the Cathedral and make your way down a choice of long stairs to the Side and then the Quayside. Stand on the bank near the Swing Bridge and imagine Ralph setting off on the errand to his mother's manager at the North Shields salt-pans, a voyage which abruptly puts an end to his easy way of life. An unlucky coincidence brings him to within sight of Tynemouth Castle on the day that the Roundhead garrison rebels and goes over to the King. Swept along on a tide of enthusiasm, and inspired by the sight of his nobleman cousin, George Selby, at the head of the mob that swarm in through the gates, Ralph finds himself enlisting in the King's cause. He soon realises the fateful and irrevocable step he has taken when the only weapon available to issue to him for the coming battle is an old scythe. The rest of the story is concerned with his fate as his selfish and safe view of the world and the people in it is shattered forever. Like his modern counterparts more than half his story lies out in the countryside.

His return to Newcastle is an ignominious one as a rebel due to be transported to the colonies or sold into the galleys of Venice. All the while, however, his once hated stepfather has been working to save his life and his escape from the Westgate Tower (via the toilet chute !) brings a temporary end to his troubles. In an afterword to the main story Ralph brings the tale up to date. His destiny proves to lie in the field of healing and to be centred overseas.

The second book is *Feast of the Serpent* – 1969 (22A – see page 26 for 22B and page 67 for 22C) in which some of the same characters appear. However, this time we start out in Northumberland with the strange pilgrimage of Adonell Heron, a girl with a gypsy mother and a border reiver father. The second half of the book begins in Newcastle with her friend Archie and his new-found importance. The help that he and his friends had given to Ralph Cole has transformed their fortunes. The author explores very closely Archie's desire to get back to his roots in the borders. This desire has been intensified by the arrival of Adonell in the town and the strange attraction that he feels for her. It is an attraction that holds true to the end of the story when he helps Adonell to survive an attempt to have her convicted and executed as a witch. Cawley's story in horrifying detail echoes the real events of 1650 when fifteen were condemned to death by hanging on the Town Moor.

The depiction of Newcastle during the Civil War in these two novels has been done largely through the author's views on the different people rather than close description of actual places. Pilgrim Street and Painter Heugh are mentioned, for example, but don't come alive as real places. She shows the Royalists and the Parliamentarians and the ideas that motivated them. She shows also those individuals who wish to shun both sides and to try to live a quiet and useful life, minding their own business. Life is often cruel and brutal but there are also many examples of honesty, kindness and compassion.

The same proves true in an even earlier visit to the Quayside in Newcastle in Barbara Leonie Picard's **_Ransom for a Knight_** – 1956 (23A – see page 95 for 23B) set in 1314.

"Bannockburn". It is a word that still means a lot to Scottish people; it recalls the one certain and unequivocal victory over the Sassenachs to the south. Bannockburn means nearly everything to young Alys de Renneville for her father and her only brother are believed to have been killed in that battle that brought freedom to the Scottish nation. In 1314 quite a few children had to get used to the painful idea of death. At least Alys is still in a comfortable home and, being the daughter of a knight, can expect a life of relative comfort and privilege. Her breeding requires her to face up to grief with courage and resolution.

Then, one day, a rider from the north brings news that her family are captives rather than slain. Unfortunately, after telling his news, the messenger loses his memory in an accident and only Alys knows the truth. Unless a ransom can be taken to Scotland her father and brother will never return home. The author has now created her plot – it is a journey northwards by Alys with the help and companionship of Hugh, a mere boy servant, in defiance of the logic of the grown-ups who are now her guardians. Concealed on her body are the jewels that will pay the ransom but which will also provide the temptation for thieves and rogues.

Eventually, of course, after many adventures the two children reach the north-east of England. By the time they reach Newcastle Alys, still determined to preserve every one of the jewels for the ransom, has been reduced to begging. She has also fallen ill and there is a moving scene on the streets of Newcastle where she is rescued from the cold and the hunger by the compassion of a cobbler's wife. For three weeks the journey is delayed in Newcastle until she is well enough to press on to Morpeth as the winter begins to close in. The climax to her story also lies amongst the wild moors of north Northumberland.

The Hoppings

Our last glimpse of the Town Moor has been grim and revolting – fourteen women and one man were put to death for the sake of superstition. But our children's writers have also provided us with a happier vision, perhaps all the happier because it seems to belong to the days of lost innocence. We have already mentioned Winifred Finlay's _The Witch of Redesdale_ and it opens with a delightful description of "the Hoppings" or, as she puts it, "the great Festival of the Town Moor" in 1950s Newcastle. Here in this first chapter, "Prologue to

The Hoppings – somehow changed but somehow still the same as in "The Witch of Redesdale".

Adventure", we can find summed up the essence of the almost "lost domains" of children's literature that are the inspiration for this little book. You can still visit the same place, you can still be a part of the crowds that throng around you, and you can still be deafened by the noise of the ceaseless stream of music from the different attractions. But you have changed as you have grown older and, in various subtle ways, the nature of the Hoppings has altered irreversibly. No longer is the air filled with "A Bicycle Made for Two", and do you think it the height of pleasure to ride a roundabout horse to the tune of "The Skater's Waltz"? Teenage girls are also highly unlikely to be interested in the patter of a huckster who is selling a patent medicine cure for colds and other ailments. It really is a world of innocence that seems to have totally disappeared. In order to enter it again you have to ignore modern attitudes and modern prejudices.

This is not that Winifred Finlay wasn't aware of the harsher realities of life for children in Newcastle. The hero of her junior Edgar Allan Poe award-winning novel *Danger at Black Dyke* – 1968 (24A – see page 71 for 24B) is Geordie, who has been rescued from the grim back-streets of Newcastle by his redoubtable grandmother. Yes, again and again in the children's books about Newcastle there is a recurring theme about the grimness of life being alleviated by surprising scenes of almost magical happiness.

A Voyage down the Ouse Burn – *Jesmond, High Heaton, Heaton and Byker*

Ballet in Jesmond

Rather than darting around the city to the various locations still to be mentioned, our best plan is now to explore both the books and the places by taking for a while a literary journey down the Ouseburn Valley, with a few short excursions to the suburbs that lie along its course. This minor stream starts its life by Newcastle Airport and then winds its way through Gosforth, Jesmond, High Heaton, Heaton and Byker to the River Tyne. A large section of the small river flows through the areas of parkland known as Jesmond Dene, which we have already touched upon in *Joe and the Magpie* and, more potently, in Aidan Chambers' *Marle.* In that book it was the haven in the city that allowed Kevin and Susan to reflect for a while on their futures away from the grim reality of earning a living. Yet in the ballet stories of Lorna Hill the middle-class suburb of Jesmond becomes a place where dreams of the future start to become a reality. In a dance studio above a terrace of shops

The dance studio in Manor House Road, Jesmond. Go through the white archway in the centre and up to the world of Lorna Hill's "Sadler's Wells" and "Dancer" stories.

and a restaurant lies "Mary Martin's" dance academy, the starting point for so many of the "Wells" heroines on their journeys to fame and fulfilment. In the "Dancer" series it is called the "Nelly Brandon" school of dancing but in reality, whilst the books were being written in the 1950s, it was the Nelly Potts school of dancing. If you go to Manor House Road you can still see the same premises being used for dancing lessons, the place where Lorna Hill's own daughter, Vicki, began her ballet career and where the fictional Jane, Sylvia, Ella, Nona, Annette, Vicki and Vanessa took their first tentative steps.

Perhaps the best homage to this special place comes in *The Little Dancer* – 1956 (25) when Annette returns to Newcastle from London on Christmas Eve in the very early morning to find snow on the streets. She walks up Grainger Street, gives a passing nod to Grey's Monument, continues up Northumberland Street, past the church with its Christmas trees in St. Mary's Place and out to Jesmond. All she wants to do is see again the studio of her youth before she blows a kiss to the building and then heads back into town as the city comes awake. In a later chapter her journey down the A1 in a blizzard is much more dramatic. With nowhere to sleep the night she and Angus press on in the hope of spending the miserable hours till dawn in the waiting room on Central Station (there again !). However, a kindly policeman takes pity on them and they actually pass the night in the cells, presumably at the police station on Market Street.

A return to Jesmond Dene at this point brings us to the story of Sylvia Swan whose family have fallen on hard times. In *Swan Feather* – 1958 (26) Sylvia and her mother are forced to leave their country vicarage and live in Coggs Road, which is one of the streets which slope steeply down to the Tyne. They live in an upstairs flat but the door is at road level. Worse than the apparent squalor of the district is the behaviour of the street gangs of young people that hang around the workings of "Benton Lane construction site". One winter's night Sylvia is nearly raped by a young hooligan who is dragging her towards a derelict house. When rescued by Peter she refuses to go to "Benton Road" police station so as not to upset her mother. Later the gang attack the house and totally vandalise it, leaving Sylvia to find her mother dead amongst the ruins. It is somewhat of a relief to learn that later the police take decisive action and clear out the gang. This sudden return to the steep streets of Scotswood and Benwell in the west end of the city takes us back to the world of Armstrong's factory. Those of an ironic turn of mind can see how easily we can go back again to Jesmond Dene, for it was the great armaments manufacturer who gave these extensive parklands to the city.

The story of Sylvia and Peter is not all sadness and ugliness. During a particularly cold winter they pass through Jesmond Dene and climb the slopes to Paddy Freeman's Park in High Heaton. There they skate on the frozen pond, and as they look back across the city they see the moon rising like a magnificent golden Chinese lantern over the nearby suburbs. The same idea of skating on Paddy Freeman's pond occurs in Winifred Finlay's

Paddy Freeman's Pond still freezes but is no longer the rendezvous for skaters that it was in "Swan Feather" and "Mystery in the Middle Marches".

Storm Over Cheviot – The story may end amongst the snowy Cheviots but it begins in the Haymarket bus station.

Mystery in the Middle Marches – 1964 (27A – see page 91 for 27B) as does a hair-raising journey by car in a blizzard to Stagshaw in the Tyne Valley. It is in this frozen park that Sylvia finds the feather which becomes the good-luck token that is to play so significant a part in her future career. But before she leaves the city there are the walks with Peter beside the stream in Jesmond Dene where he teeters on the brink of a marriage proposal that would have changed both of their lives.

More of the Lorna Hill "Wells" books explore the different possibilities of the suburbs and the city. The least pleasant is the world of suburbia suggested by the district of Hayfield (probably meant to be High Heaton) in ***Rosanna Joins the Wells*** – 1956 (28). Life in a semi-detached villa on "Denton Drive" is made to seem dull, conformist and lacking in inspiration, the very idea of a garden overlooked by someone else being somehow distasteful. It is in this same book that Timothy Roebottom, who gained his degree at Newcastle University, tells himself that he could never ask a ballet dancer like Ella Rosetti to share her life with him in a "grey, industrial, northern city". Rosanna herself determines to earn money by dancing for the amusement of the people in the Theatre Royal queue on a Saturday afternoon whilst the police are pre-occupied with a football match at St. James' Park.

Later in ***Dress Rehearsal*** – 1959 (29) the author tells the story of Nona, born under one of the bridges of the Tyne, who is brought up in an institution for homeless children in another unidentified district of Newcastle and who is bullied by the fellow inmates until rescued by a tough urchin of the streets who has a heart of gold.

The Garage in Heaton

A little further down the Ouse Burn in Heaton it is possible to climb out of the Dene and make our way to Westwood Avenue, just off Chillingham Road. In particular you can still walk down the wide back alley and try to spot the garage that was the inspiration for David Almond's Carnegie Medal and Whitbread Book of the Year winning ***Skellig*** – 1999 (30). This is another story so recently printed that it is best savoured at first hand. Sufficient to say that all the potentials for distress and tragedy lie ready at hand to overwhelm the young boy who has just moved with his family into a new home. In the garage, however, is something else that from unpromising beginnings will transform the whole of his world. David Almond wanted to make his readers feel that it could happen to any boy and girl anywhere, but the fact remains the idea came to him in that house in Heaton.

Below the Bridges in Byker

After the Ouse Burn passes below the lower acres of Heaton Park (another gift from the mighty Lord Armstrong) it eventually plunges under the massive culvert constructed in the 1920s to emerge into a totally different environment in the district of Byker. Here we are back in the industrial wasteland that can lie in the heart of any big city. Eventually it will be transformed by the coming redevelopment but for the moment it is no more than a dirty tidal sluice leading to the river. One further mention of Winifred Cawley's ***Feast of the Serpent*** (22B – see page 21 for 22A and page 67 for 22C) does not improve the atmosphere. You can still stand at the site of the Glasshouse Bridge that used to be there at the time of the Civil War and which in its modern incarnation is still the last bridge before the Tyne. In her chilling account of the abominable witchcraft trials Winifred Cawley makes it the place where one of the accused, the simple-minded Kattren Welsh, found her tame thrush which she called Lillico. Inevitably it was regarded as her "familiar" creature and the sure proof of her guilt. You may laugh at this nonsense but remember – she hanged anyway.

Climb up on to the modern Upper Glasshouse Bridge and you can look down the river to see the bends of the Tyne that were followed by the German bombers which we shall meet again in Robert Westall's account of Tynemouth during the Second World War. Look up the City Road in the other direction and you can see St. Ann's Church which survived a downpouring of German incendiaries, though the houses nearby were not so lucky. It is one of the possible models for All Saints Church in Philip Turner's "Darnley Mills" stories,

Where the Ouse Burn meets the Tyne lie the Upper and Lower Glasshouse Bridges.

often thought to be in Yorkshire but which the author himself said consisted of an imaginary land that stretched to the Scottish Border. In **Dunkirk Summer** – 1973 (31) he tells the tale of three young people fighting to save the old church in the north-east as the Luftwaffe attempts to destroy the industries and port facilities that lie nearby.

However, to be absolutely sure of being in Newcastle during the war, we have to turn again to Lorna Hill and her story called **Northern Lights** – 1999 (32). The children are passing through on their way to a destination well away from the bombs, in north Northumberland. They arrive in Newcastle by car as night falls. Walking on the city centre streets under the black-out is described as "a new and weird experience". They grope their way up Grainger Street and go in through the "screened and light-trapped doors" of Fenwicks. After purchasing their presents they emerge on to the pavement thoroughly confused. They had intended to come out on to Northumberland Street but, like so many people before and after them, they found themselves at the Blackett Street entrance. More baffled wandering eventually gets them to the Haymarket just as their bus is about to leave. But the wartime buses are different. Lights are covered by thick blue shades and the windows are three quarters painted out with thick black paint. They set off into the darkness.

A different kind of darkness provides the climactic scene in **The Secret** – 1964 (33). We retrace our steps a while to pay a last visit to the lower Ouse Burn. In this final book of her long "Wells" series Lorna Hill makes full use of the contrast between the world of industrial Tyneside and the life of the rural gentry. What possible connection could there be between the girl brought up by the minor aristocrats out in the country and Sam, the boy from the world of Brewery Terrace under Byker Bridge ? That is the "secret" that gradually unfurls during the course of the story. Two images from Lorna Hill's descriptions stick in your mind. She declared it was perfectly possible to stand on Byker Bridge and drop a stone on to the roof of the terrace where Sam had his bedroom. The Ship Inn at the head of Lime Street is the only building that is in the right place for this today. Even more compelling are the thoughts that rush through the head of the heroine, Vanessa, as she stands on the bridge in the middle of the thick fog, and gazes down into what she thinks of as a "witch's cauldron" as the fumes of the brewery and the paint factory drift up to her. To find the answer to the mystery that has shrouded her life she must go down into this dark, frightening "other" world. Her fears prove justified for she is chased through the maze of half-demolished houses and derelict factories by the wild and malicious O'Leary boys. Lurking around each corner, it seems, are the dirty and threatening waters of the Ouse Burn and then the Tyne. The rescue, when it comes, is all the more satisfactory. From our point of view it is also fortuitous, for the story ends with the secret still safe and with Sam and Vanessa's journey through foggy Byker into the centre of town and back once again to the start of our journey on the platforms of Newcastle Central Station.

It is time for Vanessa to leave to fulfil her destiny; it is time for us to move out of Newcastle and see the rest of the children's story world that lies north of the Tyne.

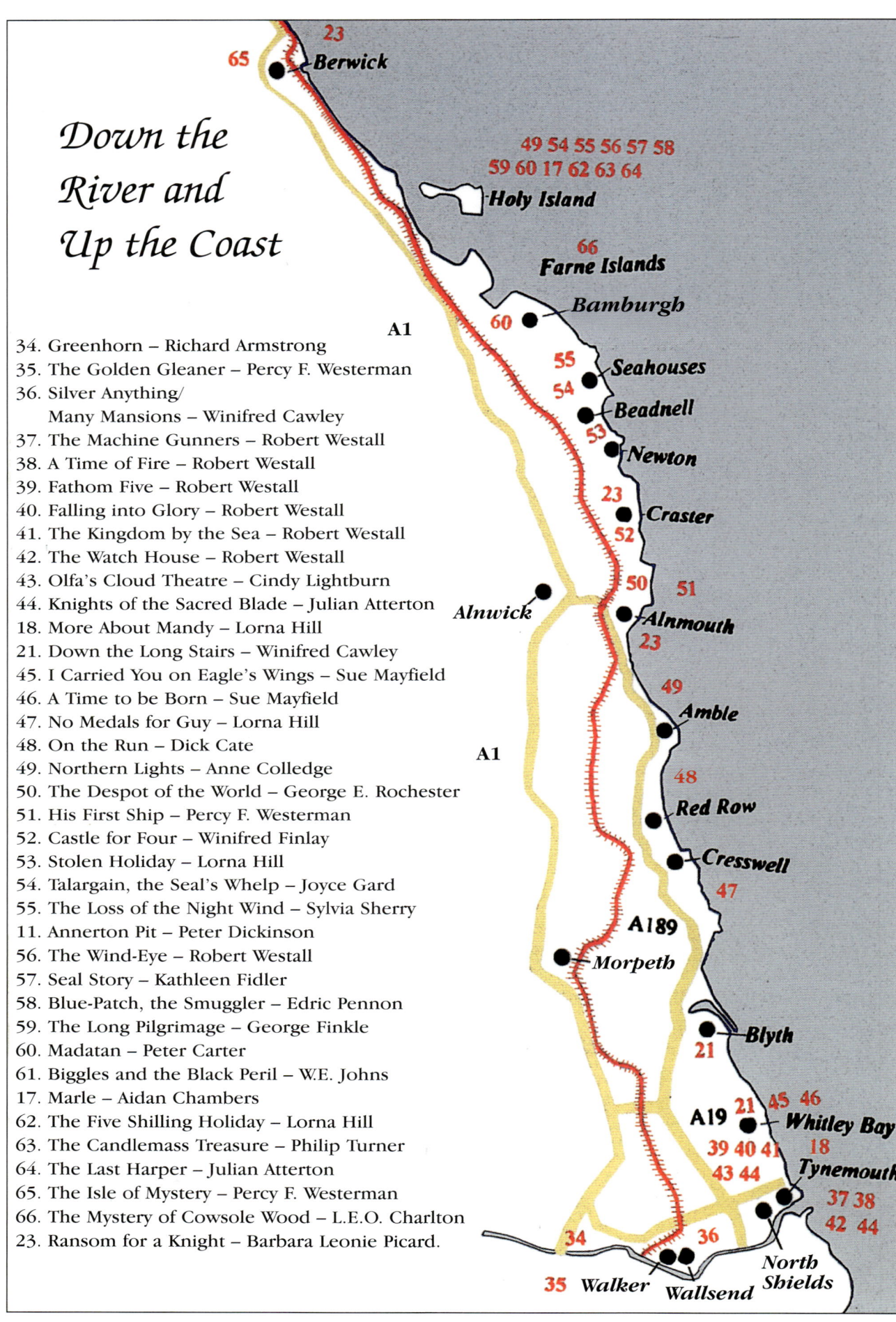

Down the River and Up the Coast

34. Greenhorn – Richard Armstrong
35. The Golden Gleaner – Percy F. Westerman
36. Silver Anything/
    Many Mansions – Winifred Cawley
37. The Machine Gunners – Robert Westall
38. A Time of Fire – Robert Westall
39. Fathom Five – Robert Westall
40. Falling into Glory – Robert Westall
41. The Kingdom by the Sea – Robert Westall
42. The Watch House – Robert Westall
43. Olfa's Cloud Theatre – Cindy Lightburn
44. Knights of the Sacred Blade – Julian Atterton
18. More About Mandy – Lorna Hill
21. Down the Long Stairs – Winifred Cawley
45. I Carried You on Eagle's Wings – Sue Mayfield
46. A Time to be Born – Sue Mayfield
47. No Medals for Guy – Lorna Hill
48. On the Run – Dick Cate
49. Northern Lights – Anne Colledge
50. The Despot of the World – George E. Rochester
51. His First Ship – Percy F. Westerman
52. Castle for Four – Winifred Finlay
53. Stolen Holiday – Lorna Hill
54. Talargain, the Seal's Whelp – Joyce Gard
55. The Loss of the Night Wind – Sylvia Sherry
11. Annerton Pit – Peter Dickinson
56. The Wind-Eye – Robert Westall
57. Seal Story – Kathleen Fidler
58. Blue-Patch, the Smuggler – Edric Pennon
59. The Long Pilgrimage – George Finkle
60. Madatan – Peter Carter
61. Biggles and the Black Peril – W.E. Johns
17. Marle – Aidan Chambers
62. The Five Shilling Holiday – Lorna Hill
63. The Candlemass Treasure – Philip Turner
64. The Last Harper – Julian Atterton
65. The Isle of Mystery – Percy F. Westerman
66. The Mystery of Cowsole Wood – L.E.O. Charlton
23. Ransom for a Knight – Barbara Leonie Picard.

Jacket illustration by William Stobbs for "Silver Everything and Many Mansions" (OUP 1976), reprinted by permission of Oxford University Press.

Stage 2: Down the River and Up the Coast

Quayside

OUR voyage down the river begins naturally enough at Newcastle Quayside. Already, in *Down the Long Stairs* by Winifred Cawley, we have heard of how young Ralph Cole sails down in the collier brig to his appointment with rebellion at Tynemouth. 300 years later a longer voyage is undertaken by the greenhorn in the book of the same name by the Carnegie medal-winning author, Richard Armstrong.

Greenhorn – 1965 (34), a short book (49 pages) in the Salamander series is the only one from Richard Armstrong's long career as a writer about the sea that touches upon Newcastle upon Tyne. It is a book written for younger children about the life amongst the apprentices on the *SS Limpopo,* a bulk carrier that, at the beginning of the story, is making ready to sail from Newcastle to Genoa. The *Limpopo* is tied up at the old Quayside and the new apprentice turns up for his first ship in two taxis, one for himself and one for his luggage. This proves to be a big mistake, for to bring so much kit marks him out as a greenhorn or total novice. Instead of his real name of Ironside being turned into his usual affectionate nickname of "Rusty" he becomes known contemptuously as "Tinribs" by one of his fellow apprentices. How the young men learn to work together and become friends is the story of the rest of the book.

Walker and Wallsend

To follow this exploration downstream we really need to resort to the eastward-bound City Road or the southern loop of the Metro system. This will soon take us to Walker and then Wallsend and the shipyards where ships of all sizes and purposes used to be built.

The Golden Gleaner – 1948 (35) by Percy F. Westerman is the story of the first voyage of one of Whatmough and Duvant's cargo ships. However, it is the account of the launching of the cargo ship in question that sets a part of the story firmly on Tyneside. The author, Percy F. Westerman, resorts to bogus details – the shipbuilders are called "Simcox and Strong" and the town where the ship is due to take to the water is "Kirby-on-Tyne". As we shall see, Westerman, born, brought up and living his entire life on the south coast of England, knew little about this part of the country but he certainly knew about ships and small boats. Thus his description of the sort of vessel turned out by a Tyneside yard at this time has the ring of truth.

The ship was due to be named the *Golden Gain* but, for some unknown reason, was changed to the *Golden Gleaner.* Inevitably this leads to the grim foreboding that she is doomed to be an unlucky ship. When she slides just six feet down the slipway and then refuses to go any further the worst suspicions of the "old shellbacks" seems to be confirmed. It is a clever piece of anti-climax when the whole ceremony has to be deferred to the next high tide the following day. All the arrangements for workers, managers and guests have to be carefully re-arranged. However, the *Golden Gleaner* spoils it all by taking matters into her own hands and, for no apparent reason, launches herself on the midnight tide. Only the weighted chains prevent her from crashing into properties on the other side of the river. The other nineteen chapters of this twenty chapter novel concern the first voyage and there is no real further connection with the north-east, except as a reference to the birth-place of the jinxed vessel.

But the story of the great shipyards and the towns that depended on them is a long and chequered one. We are fortunate indeed to have the semi-autobiographical stories of Winifred Cawley to bring them to life as they were in the 1920s.

In *Silver Everything* and *Many Mansions* – 1976 (36) the reader is given a vision of the world of the Tyneside back-streets as seen through the eyes of an eight-year old girl. Jinnie Friend is both sensitive and intelligent but, like any child at any time, struggles to come to terms with the complexities of the world around her. Both books were clearly inspired by the author's early life in Wallsend and, because they are meant to reflect real experience, they are basically plotless though not without a storyline. Jinnie's Dad is laid off from work in the shipyards and decides to take over a small shop which is on a road not far from the high street. The details of the shift from Pilgrim Buildings to Stratford Street are described with convincing thoroughness. This means a whole new environment for Jinnie and her little brother, Robbie, to get used to. Fitting in with the children who play out in the street is the first problem. Jinnie knows that she has to find that right balance between being "a cut above" and being "common". Remaining the former would isolate her from her potential playmates and becoming the latter would bring down the wrath of her parents.

With clear precision Winifred Cawley shows you that even in the world of Tyneside working class streets there are careful gradations of affluence and respectability. Even the two railway lines are used to indicate moral superiority and inferiority. The Riverside Line, the "Low Line" because it doesn't have an embankment, is sometimes called "The Methodist Line" because it doesn't have trains on a Sunday. In contrast the "High Line", though closer to the smarter shops of the centre of town, always brings up suggestions of wickedness and indulgence. The remoteness of this world of the past from the world of most children today is perhaps brought out most strongly by attitudes to religion. Mr. Friend, Jinnie's father, is a pillar of the Chapel and he has a rigid set of attitudes to so many things that are important to the everyday world of the child. Even taking satisfaction in her success at school becomes regarded as the sin of pride. Looking closely at interesting people is condemned as the even worse vice of "Staring". Jinnie's mother, less strict, sympathetically tolerant of the weaknesses of her fellow men and women, is more of a comforting presence, even though she normally backs her husband to the hilt.

Drinking and idleness and getting goods on "tick" were a part of the everyday lives of some of the customers of the little shop. Mr. Friend may have moved up in the world by leaving behind manual work and becoming a shopkeeper but he has moved into a less respectable part of the town. Little wonder that Jinnie's life and worries about the future become bound up with her father's declining enthusiasm for the venture into which he has sunk all his savings. Before moving to Wallsend he had been a servant in a rich household and had travelled just enough to make him assume an air of knowledge about the current political situations. At heart he is a kind and compassionate man but he seems to be annoyed that he is living in an uncertain world of declining standards.

The most vivid chapters of Jinnie's initiation into life in the new street come in her encounters with Mollie Molloy, the girl who is required to help the family finances by collecting horse-muck in a smelly home-made barrow. Sheer bad luck ensures that Jinnie gets off on the wrong foot with the older girl and a period of intensive bullying occurs. This culminates in a quite revolting incident involving the horse-muck. When Jinnie emerges on the other side of her ordeal she finds that she has been accepted into the normal world of the street and the school. In the second of the stories *Many Mansions*, which joins seamlessly to the first, Jinnie has two contrasting adventures or experiences. Firstly she enters into the high-spirited warfare between two rival gangs of girls and ends up giving a black eye to the daughter of the local policeman. She decides to run away from justice and takes refuge in her old environment back down in Pilgrim's Buildings. Secondly she travels with her father into Newcastle, along Scotswood Road on a tram and out into the Tyne Valley to the decaying mansion where her father had once been in service. It had come to represent some form of golden age to him but the visit is enough to ensure that he realises that his future lies with his small shop. He too has understood that there is no running away.

One of the best sections of the book is where Jinnie listens to her mother being persuaded by a Jewish travelling salesman into making her shop branch out into clothing

Alnmouth – George Rochester's "The Despot of the World". "Day is almost done, and the shades of the coming night are creeping in across the restless sea to swathe in grey shadow the silent dunes of sand".

Dunstanburgh Castle – In "Stolen Holiday" by Lorna Hill there's a mystery about the shadowy occupants of this ruined stronghold by the sea.

supplies for women. Winifred Cawley traces very effectively the ebb and flow of the salesman's "patter" as he manipulates her into agreeing. This is then followed by an intriguing account of Jinnie's mother's own stubbornness and resolution as she brings her husband reluctantly round to her point of view on the subject of women's stockings. By the end of the book the new idea is proving successful and, though it is certainly not the turning point in the family's fortunes, there are signs that they are prepared to face the future with more optimism.

North Shields and Tynemouth

We travel down the river a little further to North Shields and Tynemouth. Again the Metro line will take you there, though you might be tempted to break your journey at Wallsend station and walk to Segedunum. It's a good way to prepare yourself for the visit to the central section of the Roman Wall which comes in Stage 3 of this book.

There seems little danger at the moment of Robert Westall's unique contribution to children's stories set in the north-east of England being either hidden or forgotten. Most of his books are still in print, there is more than one website devoted to his works and North Tyneside Council have even named a road in his honour. You can take a "virtual tour" of the location of many of his tales without even leaving your chair. His place in the region's literary heritage seems secure. When you add in the fact that large numbers of north-eastern schoolchildren have had *The Machine Gunners* set in front of them as their class reader during their early teenage years there seems little more that can be added here. Yet no guide to the region's authors and stories would be complete without some identification of his qualities and, it has to be said, without expressing some reservations about just exactly for whom he was writing.

The Machine Gunners – 1975 (37) was in the first instance, as Westall declared on many occasions, written for his son Chris in order to tell him just what it was like to live through the Second World War as a child. The details of everyday life under the flight-path of the German bombers were all grippingly authentic. Westall clearly remembered what people did, what people said, what people ate and what people felt like. The wartime Tyneside he creates is overwhelmingly convincing, even to the point where the idea of the children treating the war as partly a game can be found acceptable. Into this powerful evocation of his past Westall builds a story which develops towards a potentially tragic conclusion, its implausibility masked by the reader's willing acceptance of the "truth" of the general situation. When interviewed Westall always readily admitted which was genuine recollection and which was artistic invention. He succeeded in blurring the borderline between these two contributions to the success of his book by his own determination that his story must move at a rapid pace and, in particular, be stripped of all unnecessary description. There would be no time for his readers to stop "suspending their disbelief" by pausing to reflect or to analyse.

Westall also declared that he found descriptions of settings "boring" in other people's books and that they would find no place in his. It is doubly ironic therefore that nowadays there is a "Robert Westall Trail" that can be followed to his most famous settings, and that a close examination of many of his books would show that his evocation of place didn't just rely on the conjuring up of atmosphere and feelings but on actual physical details. He was in fact denying one of his own best qualities.

Another feature of his writing that should not be underestimated is his ability to present convincing moral dilemmas for his characters to face without resorting to too much undue contrivance. This is perhaps best seen in the ending of *The Machine Gunners* where Rudi, the downed German airman, makes the crucial move that ends the conflict. The feelings that Chas and the gang have for him and that he has for them are seemingly inexplicable, except to the reader who has witnessed all the gang has gone through. The British adults in the story simply cannot see what has been happening. The need to explain and to sort into acceptable categories of behaviour is neatly summed up by:

"All the adults were already busy, tidying up things in their minds, making them into more comfortable shapes."

The same adult acceptance of moral and emotional ambiguity comes at the end of the posthumously published *A Time of Fire* – 1994 (38) where Sonny finally has the opportunity to avenge the deaths of both his mother and father. The German pilot, incapacitated by drink, has stumbled into the water-filled trench and is destined to drown. Sonny saves him not because he has a change of heart towards the enemy he has good reason to hate, but because he fears the nightmares that will come if he spoils the happy refuge that his grandparents' house and garden has become for him.

At the end of *Fathom Five* – 1979 (39), originally with a different hero but presented in paperback as the sequel to *The Machine Gunners,* Chas has to make a decision about the German spy that only he can identify. The reasons for his decision are a confused whirlwind of contempt for conventional authority, the dislike of petty Tory officials and the feeling that retribution is a pointless and ultimately self-destructive impulse. As we might expect, Westall makes no attempt at a glib explanation to the complicated and challenging issues that he has presented. He leaves us to explore our own reactions to the dilemma and the choices that we might have made. However, *Fathom Five* presents us with another problem that has no easy answer. Is it really written for children ? One of the adjectives often applied by critics to Robert Westall's writing is the word "gritty". On this occasion the "grittiness" doesn't just refer to the honest representation of the language used by working-class people in times of stress, nor to the downright realistic and sometimes repulsive portrayal of the results of war. This time there is a continuing preoccupation with sexual matters. On the one hand the book would seem to slot into the "young adult" section of the market with Chas discovering his physical attraction for Sheila and the confusion and excitement of their first tentative encounters. There is also a certain amount of "Boys' Own" naïvety in the plot to identify and capture the spy who is sending British ships to their deaths. However, there is a prolonged foray into the world of prostitutes, including the possibility of a potential rape, and Chas even forms a friendship with and sympathy for the chief "madame" of the district. Strong stuff indeed unless the readership is at the appropriate age.

Falling into Glory – 1993 (40) about the affair between a sixth-former and a 32 year old teacher could certainly be read by older teenagers but is strongly adult in its exploration of themes and feelings. Both books have plenty of interesting things to say and twists and turns of plot that capture our attention but are not easy to classify as merely "children's stories".

The Kingdom by the Sea – 1990 (41) is more deliberately a children's book and takes us back to the territory first explored in *The Machine Gunners.* Robert Westall declared that he constructed it out of a rag-bag of ideas and memories that had been lying around for years. Again he appears to play down his own artistry, for he succeeded in turning these unimpressive scraps of information into a picture of the wartime north-east that seems hauntingly realistic. When his author's imagination shaped this story into a form of journey or pilgrimage he was able to use the full potential of what he had had in store for so long. From the claustrophobia of the "Garmouth" (Tynemouth) stories of *The Machine-Gunners* and *Fathom Five* the reader escapes on a voyage to the north with Harry and the dog that he finds.

The bombing raids have left Harry alone in the world, unwilling to be claimed by his aunt Elsie, after the death of his parents. There is nothing to hold him in Garmouth and he sets off walking to the north alongside the sea. Thereafter follows a series of adventures that reveal both the positive and negative sides of human nature. Genuine friendliness from some soldiers, for example, is followed by an attempted assault by a paedophile. After each encounter Harry has learned a little more about the world around him and about how he can cope with it. This knowledge is both about the practicalities of obtaining food and shelter and, more importantly, about what he wants from the world – what it will take to make him happy. When he discovers Mr. Murgatroyd and finds what he can accept as a home, Harry begins to think that his journey is complete. However, Westall still has a surprise in store that it would be unfair to reveal. Every little town on the coast between Tynemouth and Holy Island is either mentioned or suggested and once again, in spite of his own resolutions, certain places are brought alive by the perceptive use of the everyday detail. Back in Garmouth the long-standing contempt for the people on the housing estate known as "The Ridges" is conveyed very clearly.

As well as his fascination with the past which has formed the core of the stories mentioned so far, Robert Westall also had a compulsion to write adventures which depended upon the interference of the supernatural into the lives of ordinary people. Again the setting for many of these stories is the north-east of England. One of these is based around the Watch House at Tynemouth, a picture of which you can click onto your computer screen or which you can actually go and visit. The idea of strong emotions from the past being sensed by someone undergoing a time of trial in the present is not an unfamiliar one in stories about the supernatural. However, the use of the Black Middens, the Priory Headland and Tynemouth Pier as the locations for the horrific events is particularly effective. The gradual revelation of just what happened to the old wrecked ship and the people on board her is developed to a formidable climax in which there is a race against time to perform a dramatic exorcism. It is not surprising that **The Watch House** – 1977 (42) was also turned into a particularly effective television serial by the BBC. It is fascinating to see how a rather dull old building and some even duller shipping records of the past were transformed into a compelling and frightening adventure by Westall's astute handling of the narrative pace and his creation of a swampingly oppressive atmosphere.

Olfa's Cloud Theatre – 2000 (43), which was written and published by Cindy Lightburn and illustrated by Chris Mabbott, is an example of why this journey to the hidden kingdoms of the region can never be called complete. For only a chance visit to Tynemouth uncovered this ten-page story of a dog and a little girl who discover a message written on the sands at Tynemouth, meet a mysterious and magical old lady and then have a cloud show in the sky outside their front window. All the profits from this enterprise in self-publishing go to north-east animal charities. Who knows how many other stories for children have been written and produced in this way? Perhaps there are other undiscovered treasures that have been sold in the many small towns across the region.

Before we turn north and begin the exploration of this kingdom by the sea we must remember Julian Atterton's tale of the times of King Stephen, **The Knights of the Sacred Blade** – 1989 (44) which is a narrative that wanders all over the north of England. One part of it contains a secret and dangerous journey that Simon, the young hero, and Catriona, one of the girls in his life, make to the priory at Tynemouth.

Lorna Hill's second story in the *The Vicarage Children* trilogy which is called **More About Mandy** (18) is most concerned with the activities of a family in the Roman Wall country. However, there is also a well-described Sunday School trip to Tynemouth and Whitley Bay which recalls some of the lost pleasures of the seaside – including some time at Tynemouth open-air pool, at the amusements of Spanish City and a bathing-beauty competition for Miss Whitley Bay.

Whitley Bay and Blyth

The story of Ralph Cole from **Down the Long Stairs** (21B – see page 20 for 21A) must now be picked up again at Tynemouth. Those who know the north-east well will recognise all the details of Ralph's escape from Tynemouth Castle down the cliff face and his flight from the coast under cover of one of the well-known "sea-frets" that are still with us today. Hunted, starving and desperate, he crawls into a hole in the ground and goes deeper and deeper. In the darkness he meets the men who are amongst the real heroes of the story – the poor pitmen of the independent collieries of North Tyneside. At first their kindness in sheltering him from the search parties of Parliamentarians is pragmatic – after all he is the son of a hostman and his mother is sure to repay their efforts by bringing them some material gain. Later, however, Archie Rede from Elsdon in the Borders shows him genuine affection and is prepared to take both time and trouble to ensure that he escapes from the area safely.

As he wanders northwards, acting as assistant to an itinerant medicine man, who is also a disguised Catholic priest, Ralph begins to learn about the harshness of life in the small communities that he visits. The irony that his preservation depends upon a group of people whose struggle to win coal and eke out their lives in misery he had previously taken for granted is now never far from his mind. In Blyth he is witness to an explosion of underground gases and helps with the recovery of the bodies. He sees the suffering of mothers and widows and reflects on the life of the poor. He has started to take some of the first steps towards becoming a man, whilst at the same time acknowledging the pain and misery he has caused his mother because of his foolishness. A sudden journey in time can next show us the parent-child relationship from an entirely different angle.

Tony's Sharp's mother has multiple sclerosis and in *I Carried You on Eagle's Wings* – 1995 (45) by Sue Mayfield he has to come to terms with the fact that she is never going to get better. All the members of the community he lives in know that any severe illness could cause complications and result in her death. He has been dealing with this situation for a long time but now, in his mid teenage years, the oppression he feels seems to be getting heavier and heavier. At home, at school, in the church on Sunday (for he is the vicar's son) people are walking around him on egg-shells, anxious to make their concern known but unable to build up any real channel of communication with Tony, who feels more and more lonely.

The story is set somewhere on the coast, perhaps near Tynemouth, Cullercoats or Whitley Bay, yet the only place the reader could identify with any degree of confidence is the fish quay in North Shields. The beach, the school playing field, the churchyard, the vicarage and, more ominously, the hospital, all have a part to play in the story but it is fair to say that the north-eastern setting does not impinge either negatively or positively on the plot. All that really matters is the proximity of the sea and the seagulls. For Tony finds a seagull with a broken wing that he is determined to rescue and give a chance of life. A subtle contrast is drawn between the uncomplaining passivity of his mother as she slips further and further away from the world and the aggressive ungratefulness of the gull which he tries to nurse back to health. When Tony himself is injured on the football field and has to have his leg put in plaster the author introduces another parallel situation that she uses to intensify the experiences which he is passing through. The tender affection of a girl at his school, Clare Sunderland, begins to release some of the bottled-up feelings that have pushed him into depression. Unlike Gary, his boyhood friend, Clare is able to confront the painful and embarrassing detail of his mother's illness, and to offer Tony the affection of which he feels starved. His father, also at the centre of this situation, maintains his grip on his emotions and even manages to retain his calm exterior during the visit of the annoying and intrusive grandmother who comes to see her dying daughter one last time. As a clergyman he is expected to cope with his time of trial.

His mother's Christian faith makes her death, painful though it is in its details, seem like a release into a better world. At the same time the recovered seagull has gained enough strength to go back to the wild. Tony's father at last breaks down and cries out for the woman he had loved and Tony can join him in his grief, just as earlier he had been unable to share his studied stoicism.

This is a moving book on a difficult subject. Though the north-east setting matters little, the writer certainly brings out well the emotional landscape of a boy struggling with the difficult concepts of love, friendship and death.

A sequel, **A Time to be Born** – 1996 (46) continues the story of Tony's life after his mother's death. The rift with Gary continues and Jody, a new friend enters his life.

Now we have reached the point where the Metro system will no longer serve us for our exploration and the string of coastal towns and villages can only be visited by car. From a map you will see that the main arteries of transport are the A1 and the A189 which both head north. A right turn off each will bring you to a series of fascinating harbours, castles and towns and then later to beaches, causeways and islands. Each place mentioned is certainly worth a visit and each takes us further away from the world of industry and high density population. Our last glimpse of it comes as we pass Blyth and Newbiggin and then Lynemouth and look back towards the south.

Cresswell

No Medals for Guy – 1962 (47) the last of the "Marjorie" stories by Lorna Hill, has the usual group of children camping out in a converted double-decker bus somewhere between Morpeth and the coast. One of their most memorable days is spent on the beach near Cresswell (nowadays just north of the Alcan smelter), at that time a village with some small pretensions to being a seaside haven. The occasion is notable for the usual appalling behaviour by Marjorie (she cuts holes in their swimming costumes) and for a sensational rescue of two small children by the intrepid Guy Charlton.

Red Row

The Cock o' the North – 1973 (48) by Dick Cate (in the book *On the Run*) is an exhilarating and inspiring story to read. It charts the running career of Chris Armstrong in the 1950s and is filled with beautifully observed sketches of the people he meets as he embarks on his quest to be a champion. Told with both zest and dry humour, the flow of the narrative seems to match the speed of one of Chris' races. With just a few sentences Dick Cate catches the mood of surging over the moors and round the peat hags, or of trotting back along the Northumberland sands at Red Row as the sun goes down and the sea stretches away to Denmark. The quiet sincerity and deep intensity of Cedric Knowles, the man who becomes Chris' trainer and friend, is developed through a short scene at Red Row as the young man learns more about the tragedies that have left this former Morpeth to Newcastle champion with his life unfulfilled.

Druridge Bay and Amble

The collection of short stories for under 10s entitled **Northern Lights** – 2000 (49) by Anne Colledge deals with the day to day life of young Matthew and his sister Poppy. Matthew has severely restricted hearing and has to use a special hearing aid in order to be able to tune in to what other people are saying. In some of the thirteen stories in this book the author makes use of this disability to underline some point in the plot or the revelation of character. However, overall Matthew mostly comes across as a normal little boy, though perhaps a little more brave and resourceful than other children.

Local people and local events play a full part in nearly all of the stories, some of which are set on the Northumberland coast. Each story has its own little plot which has usually been woven very plausibly around aspects of Northumbrian life that occasionally make the headlines. Thus Matthew in the very first story tries to distract the famous Freddie the dolphin in Amble harbour whilst the bomb disposal experts tow a mine out to sea for disposal by controlled explosion. A journey to Holy Island is followed (inevitably) by the story of a car theft which ends on the famous causeway and, later, a trip to the Farne Islands involves a man getting lost in the mist on Inner Farne.

In different tales Matthew and Poppy are involved in the rescue of both an oiled seal (on the sands of Druridge Bay) and a little group of trapped ducklings. With the help of adults from the wildlife refuges these creatures are nursed back to health and, where possible, released back into the wild.

Every now and then details of the overall family situation are gradually released to the young reader, and, though they never dominate any one tale, these snippets of information about the dad who has moved away, and the special therapy that Matthew has to have for school, certainly do bind the collection together as one coherent whole. At times the stories stray into the area of traditional children's adventure stories. However, it also quite clear that the author also wants her readers to start thinking about some of the complex issues that face us all as we get older. Matthew dearly wants to join the local boys' football team. However, he is not in favour of a new road project that will give the community a by-pass and a new football pitch but at the expense of a stretch of land where a quite rare orchid grows. If he keeps quiet he can easily be accepted but he knows he must speak out. How he finds the courage to suggest his own solution introduces on a very simple level the notion of compromise replacing confrontation as a way of solving problems. The same thoughtful approach is shown in the last story in the book where the grandad is in peril in his fishing boat and Matthew and Poppy come to realise that the most valuable gifts in life are the relationships that we have with each other.

Alnmouth

When Sir Arthur Conan Doyle had reached the end of his tether with writing the "Sherlock Holmes" stories he killed off his hero by sending him over the Reichenbach Falls in a death-grip with his arch-enemy Professor Moriarty, the emperor of crime. George E. Rochester, the most popular writer of boys' aeroplane adventures of the 1920s and early 1930s, used much the same idea but took it a stage further. The intrepid pilot, Harry Davies, known popularly as "The Flying Beetle", was the hero of several books in which he battled evil regimes all over the world. In *The Despot of the World* (50) Rochester decided that it was time that his hero made the ultimate sacrifice.

Most of his stories were first published as serials in the "Boys' Own" paper, coming out in weekly instalments, and Rochester constantly topped the polls when the editors questioned their readers about whose stories they most wanted to see in their magazine. Just occasionally this sort of "factory writing" produces a story that rises head and shoulders above the rest. The success of *The Despot of the World* (1936 in book form but 1930 in magazine serial) is achieved through its tone. From the very beginning it is one of impenetrable sadness. The reader knows that, whatever difficulties are overcome and whatever triumphs are achieved, death awaits the hero. The story is told through the words of Major Beverley, Harry Davies' friend. And the story begins in Alnmouth, the place where Rochester himself was born.

"Day is almost done, and the shades of the coming night are creeping in across the restless sea to swathe in grey shadow the silent dunes of sand."

These are the opening words that capture at once the bitter, brooding melancholy of Beverley's narrative as he recalls the death of his friend. In his mind what happened to Harry Davies was reminiscent of the quests of the Grail Knights; it is in itself an epic of medieval proportions that is both glorious and tragic. Even the language seems to belong to the same dream and nightmare world as Coleridge's "Rhyme of the Ancient Mariner" or Browning's "Childe Rowland to the Dark Tower Came".

"As I sit here by my window I see again in the deepening dusk that strange fantastic company of Castle Grim. They pass before me, a phantom host, but I can name them all:

the cruel and merciless Zanderberg, warped of mind and body, yet brilliant of wit; the gentle Guillame, scarred by the knout, crippled by the fetters, yet with the hint of gallant laughter in his weary eyes; the brutal Borsage....."

As the narrator drifts into his dream of the past, he takes the reader with him until all the thoughts of the sad storyteller in his lonely house on a quiet misty evening in Alnmouth begin to group around his "familiar friend" and the adventure that was "the most perilous and the most tragic of them all." Then, with a dramatic change of atmosphere, Rochester uses a different vision of Northumberland weather to plunge us into the last adventure. The captain of a ship that has just docked in Amble sets off on the six mile walk in the middle of the night to deliver the message that is to summon Beverley to Russia. Lashed by the wind and pelted by the gale, he arrives at the remote house where it seems the breakers will surely smash down the front door. The letter is delivered and the narrator sets off on the first stage of the long, perilous journey that will take him to his comrade. And, at the end of the book, in a twist of the plot that it would be unfair to reveal, he witnesses the sacrifice that is both so wonderfully upsetting and tragically uplifting

Thus Rochester's recreation of Alnmouth in two contrasting moods is the starting point for one of the classic "Boys' Own" adventures. The bulk of the action may lie elsewhere but his memories of his Northumberland childhood gave Rochester the inspiration to create the brooding, melancholy atmosphere that works so well in this strange story.

Two ironic notes must follow.

Rochester was eventually outstripped in popularity by that other well-known writer of flying stories: Captain W.E.Johns. Both men were shot down whilst on active service in the First World War and, most remarkably, both men were placed for a while in the same German prison camp.

And, Harry Davies, the Flying Beetle – what became of Rochester's most famous creation ? No sooner was he dead than the call came for the author to bring him back to life. It was the story of Sherlock Holmes all over again and Rochester duly complied with his readers' demands.

All at Sea

The author Percy F. Westerman is practically unknown today but he was voted the most popular writer for boys by the English Library service back in the early 1930s. His output was prodigious, with over 176 full-length books and many other serials and short stories in popular boys' magazines and comics. Most of his stories were about the adventures of boys and young men in the merchant navy, boys on holidays by the seaside, and recruits in the air police and the air force. He wrote a mixture of books with characters who only appeared in that one story and "series" books interlinked by either the main characters or the organisation to which they belonged. Thus the fictional shipping firm of "Whatmough and Duvant" embraces several generations of ships' officers who serve all over the world. A boy who appears as a humble cadet in one story might pop up thirty years later as the awe-inspiring ship's captain. With such a prolific level of production it is hardly surprising that the quality of what Westerman wrote was very variable. Quite promising but still slim in its information is the experience of Alan Carr in *His First Ship* – 1936 (51) who makes his first voyage from Boston in Lincolnshire up to Scotland. As he copes with sea-sickness he gazes out of the scuttle.

"He could see the Durham coast – a mass of tall chimneys from which smoke was pouring. Industry was reviving on the Tyne and although all the factories weren't working there were far more than in the year of the recent slump."

This bland and conventional description does little more than repeat a cliché about the north-east. However, almost immediately, Westerman gives an entirely compelling vision of what it is like to effect a rescue in the pounding seas off Alnmouth. A disabled yacht is taken in tow but then abandoned when all efforts to keep her afloat prove futile. The details of what the ship's crew have to do in the terrific seas of the north-east fishing grounds to save the amateur yachtsman amply compensate for any earlier lack of information about the land lying to the west. The distressed seamen are landed at Berwick and the *S.S. Mary Rumbold* proceeds on her voyage and Alan Carr sets out on his career. Carr is in fact Westerman's most long-lived series hero and we follow his progress through different books until he finally achieves command.

Craster

A quick consideration of two more of Winifred Finlay's north-eastern books confirms that the theme of boys and girls learning to live with each other in friendship instead of antipathy is one that the writer cared deeply about. She is exploring a stage in their development that comes before romantic or sexual attraction. It is a stage where boys within their own world are inclined to treat outsiders with suspicion or hostility. Even elder brothers or sisters are merely personalities on the margin, tolerated because their supervision, less rigorous than the usual parental dictatorship, is often subverted by yearning after the opposite gender. Thus in **Castle for Four** – 1966 (52) the younger brother Rickie discovers that he has unprecedented power because Paul is at the stage where a letter from a possible girlfriend dominates his thoughts. The irony is that Rickie himself finds that he is the focus of attention for young Lesley who has been starved of any sort of juvenile company during her formative years. How Rickie gradually comes to understand, appreciate and then enjoy Lesley's friendship is cleverly compared and contrasted with the broken relationship between old John Grey and Sheila Fenwick who parted on the eve of the Second World War. For those who know and love the Northumberland coast there are many splendid scenes in *Castle for Four* which can be visualised even today. A chance encounter at Bamburgh Castle leads to the remarkable opportunity for Rickie to spend his summer holiday in an old castle on the coast.

Go to Craster and, instead of following the well-trodden route to Dunstanburgh, turn south and be on the look-out for where you would place the old ruined peel tower that is the site of Winifred Finlay's Cushat Castle. Study the rock face and imagine the old smuggler's cave that some believe is the entrance to an underground passage that leads inland to a dilapidated manor house. Inevitably Lesley and Rickie think of a Cushat Castle smuggler's route that is still being used by modern day criminals. Ultimately, just as in Finlay's *Danger at Black Dyke,* the promising tunnel really leads nowhere; however, in both cases the present-day children learn that other young people before them have explored and hoped in the same way. There is a connection between the generations in the dangers that they run and the friendships that they form. Rickie and Lesley see the old romance between John Grey and Sheila Fenwick begin to be rekindled. The tunnels may have come to a dead end but new and more exciting relationships have been opened up.

Newton-by-the-Sea, Beadnell

The second "Marjorie" story by Lorna Hill, entitled **Stolen Holiday** – 1948 (53) is amongst her best, with the children staying in one of the beach bungalows at Beadnell and developing their usual rows and strange alliances. Midnight bathing in ice-cold seas, a cliff accident on the Farne Islands, a mystery connected with Dunstanburgh Castle, a travelling fair in Seahouses, the slaughter of animals near Bamburgh and, best of all (or should that be worst of all ?) Marjorie ending the book by behaving so badly that she gets expelled from "The Clan".

Seahouses

In her preface to **Talargain, the Seal's Whelp** – 1964 (54) the author, Joyce Gard, declares that Lucilla's town is not Seahouses but the rest of the book, both the section set in the present and that set in the 7th century, confirms by the discussion of its geography and its heritage that this declaration is only a form of retreat into a half-world where things might be true or they might be fantasy. The first seven chapters of the book, detailing the modern-day Lucilla's return to the north and the home of her mother's family, and her fascination with the sea and with the seals that swim near the Farnes, are only a prelude to the mystic story of Talargain that fills every other page. Inspired by the old tales of the affinity between seals and men and by the stories about the early Christian saint, Cuthbert, Joyce Gard creates her own myth about the young man who comes from the sea to tell his story to Lucilla, the red-haired girl of the modern town.

Talargain's story unfolds slowly as he talks of the way he came to the knowledge of himself and his heritage. At first he believed he was the son of Red Brock and the twin of Angharad, the product of an Angle father and a Celtic mother. An early fight with Garulf, the boy who as a man is to become his deepest enemy, leaves him with the knowledge that there is something mysterious about his parentage. Though secure in the love of what he now knows is his foster family, Talargain feels drawn to other people and to swimming with the seals in the sea. It is the famous St. Cuthbert who is his godfather. It was Cuthbert, the lover and protector of the animals on Farne, who had saved him and his dying mother from the sea and who had passed him as a baby to Morwen who became his new mother.

Whilst he is growing to maturity Talargain's own story becomes dwarfed by the wars between the kingdoms around him. King Ecgfrith of Northumbria wants to make war on the Pictish people to the north and sets off with his army into the hills on his borders. All Cuthbert's injunctions about Christian peace have no impact on the warlike lord of Bamburgh. Meanwhile Talargain is reaching maturity and, in spite of his admiration for the community on Holy Island and his marvelling at the beautiful book of the Gospel of St. Mark that he sees soon after its creation, he realises that the life of a monk is not for him. It is with the seals that he feels most at home, swimming in his especially-made seal costume and being befriended by his special seal companions: Calypso, Proteus and Wayland.

Disaster strikes King Ecgfrith and he and most of his men are killed in an ambush in the Scottish Hills. A new king, Aldfrith, a distant half-nephew, is invited to take power and he proves a very different character from his predecessor. Talargain is taken into his confidence and is soon sent on a very special mission to the north. Little does he know that he carries not only the fate of his country but also the key to his own destiny when he begins his journey to the fearsome King Bridei of the Picts.

It is perhaps this concept of the messenger that contains the most interesting idea of the book. Joyce Gard presents King Aldfrith as a visionary who has a picture in his mind of the kingdom of Britain with all the warring factions at peace – a harmonious country where boundaries are fixed and where each lord can concentrate on helping his people with tilling the soil and raising the animals. The stock of the people, already partially interbred, would become even stronger by further mixing of the bloods in the time of harmony. Even the fearsome Bridei recognises the worthiness of Aldfrith's idea but prophetically remarks "Not in my time".

The book ends amongst a rush of action with plague, the destructiveness of superstition, the loss of hope over a shipwreck, the malevolence of disappointed men and the marvels of return, rescue and the miraculous intervention of the seals.

The modern-day Lucilla has been able to hear Talargain's tale because she has that special gift of "seeing". She has been drawn to his spirit which returns to that particular stretch of coast because of his love for the shape of the grass, the touch of the sand and the flight of the birds. She even catches a glimpse of the image of the girl who became Talargain's bride and returned to the sea and the seals with him.

It was clearly Joyce Gard's intention to take the real sights and sounds of this part of the Northumberland coast and the offshore islands and to blend them in her tale with aspects of real history and old legends and myths. For, if she told her tale well enough, we too could receive the message and become "seers", ready to live in harmony with the places, the living creatures and our fellow human beings.

The Loss of the Night Wind – 1970 (55) by Sylvia Sherry, on the other hand, is a story which is firmly set in the real world of the fishing community on the north-east coast.

Sylvia Sherry calls her fictional port Rudharbour. It is most likely based on Seahouses, though it shares some features with Craster and Amble. Perhaps the crucial factor in allocating the final decision to Seahouses is the nearness of Lindisfarne or Holy Island. The traditional story device of having a family as "incomers" to a small community is deployed very effectively in this first person narrative. The energy of the story-line is provided by the way in which young John Watt grapples with the ways of the village and the mysteries that lie in its past. Only by understanding the local way of life and the relationships between the rugged people who treat him as an interfering kid can he hope to solve the mystery of the loss of the "Night Wind", a small fishing boat that has apparently sunk, causing the death of its crew of three.

Life in the community is far from idyllic. This is not a holiday adventure story for younger children. There is an uncompromising bleakness about both the people and the landscape. The book actually opens with the determination of John's friend, Fordie Telford, to run away because he is sick of the place which he regards as a "dump". John's own father is an ex-miner who ekes out his existence on a compensatory pension determined that his only son shall be neither "buried" down the mine nor "buried" at sea. Overall there is a sense of tiredness and of closed-off bitterness that has infected the whole village. John himself is a bird-watcher, a close observer and a methodical chronicler of all the wildlife he sees. He has formed an unlikely alliance with an old, half-crazed, man who lives in a shack on Holy Island.

When the "Night Wind" goes missing during a period of extremely calm weather it seems that John has lost his friend Fordie for ever. The village is convinced that Fordie has gone down with the missing ship. A short but effective description of the grief of Fordie's grandmother intensifies the claustrophobic and doom-laden atmosphere that surrounds John. However, together with the local coastguard, he tries to piece together the movements of the small fishing fleet and the other boats that were off the coast of Northumberland on the night that the tragedy happened. Just as John begins to unravel how the bitter feelings and mistrust in the village are all connected with a previous disaster, the loss of the "Northern Maid", his attention is claimed by the demands of Holy Joe from Lindisfarne who declares that something has crawled out of the sea that he must come and look at. The reader then realises that the solution to the whole mystery does lie in both the hidden past of the village and in what has dragged itself on to the sand of Holy Island. John suddenly leaps to the correct conclusion about how and where the "Night Wind" was dragged under. His deductions about who was responsible are not so sound and he places several lives in danger as the culprit attempts once again to cover up what he has done.

The crossing to Holy Island and the dangers caused by the incoming tide have stirred many people's imagination. In this book Sylvia Sherry uses all the dramatic potential of the ordinary processes of nature to enhance the climax of her book. As the waves rush towards the causeway so the killer closes in on his next victims.

Apart from the fictionalised idea of Rudharbour, which has the real attributes of many small Northumberland ports, all the other details of landscape and waterscape ring true. It would be possible on a map to trace the movements of the boats involved or thought to be involved. The characters of the fishermen are skilfully created, though the conspiracy of silence about past events is only acceptable when you remember that the narrator is a fourteen year old boy and still an outsider to the small community. A constant running theme in the book has been the nature of the bird-life and its relationship with the habitat and the people of the coast. The author refers again and again to the noise of the seagulls who scavenge for food around the edge of the community. John's precise study of the migrating birds confirms what Holy Joe had said to him all the time. Their progress and the way they can be drawn off course has mirrored what has happened to John himself during this vital period of growth to maturity. Unlike *Dark River, Dark Mountain* which ends on a sad and bitter note for the Newcastle born hero who has become a rootless wanderer, "The Loss of the Night Wind" has brought John Watt to a greater understanding of and identity with the place where he will grow up.

It is time to pick up the story again of the blind boy who comes to Newcastle on the back of his brother's motorbike. *Annerton Pit* (11B – see page 14 for 11A) is, of course, a fictional creation. It is located "somewhere beyond Alnwick" on the coast. Peter Dickinson incorporates the features that one expects to find in a typical Northumbrian mine by having a local expert give a catalogue of what Jake and Martin can expect to find when they get there. A small drift mine where the coal was quarried by tracing a seam sideways into the hillside is followed by a vertical shaft mine when the lie of the coal deposits is found to be interrupted by a fault line. As no natural harbour exists a protective haven is built so that quick and easy export can maximise the profit for the coal owners. A waste tip grows to dominate the village and this eventually leads to the great disaster and the tales of the haunting. More than a hundred years have passed since the end of the pit but the stories of "something" coming out of the rock still persist.

Not unexpectedly, the core of the story takes place in the remains of the pit. Certainly, there is a plot about eco-warriors who are conspiring to take violent action in order to preserve the planet from despoliation, but the "green" issue is very much subservient to the story of Jake's desperate exploration of the smells, textures and temperatures of the half-drowned, wind-riddled tunnels and channels that may or may not lead to the surface.

Though a blind boy is not afraid of the darkness, Jake discovers that there is something there to fear. It is something that cannot be explained away by his grandfather's healthy scepticism or the history lessons he has learned at school. Whether it is a creature of the depths, or the sudden realisation of the different layers of contradictory feeling lying within all of us, is never concluded. It is true to say that Peter Dickinson in *Annerton Pit* tries to make us feel the physical reality of a pit, experienced through all our senses, and, alongside this, he uses the underground exploration as a remarkable metaphor for how we put ourselves in touch with our own deepest feelings.

Holy Island

The Wind-Eye by Robert Westall – 1976 (56) is less rigorously structured and less finely focused than his earlier *The Watch House,* though the author's imagination again impresses by the way in which he has blended past and present in a tale which offers unlimited potential for mysterious happenings and complex ideas. This time the happenings all take place on the Northumberland coast, Holy Island and the Farne Islands. The dysfunctional Studdard family of the present day encounter the "Resurre", an ancient boat that can somehow travel through time and transport them back to the world of ancient Christianity and the realm of St. Cuthbert. As a result of this contact each member of the family changes, though a certain lack of clarity in the constant explanations offered leaves the reader impressed by the mysticism rather than the logic of Westall's narrative. But the author himself, through the relentless shattering of the composure of the character of the atheistic father, Bernard, tries to make the reader realise that any scepticism will always be defeated by the inexplicable nature of faith.

More books about the north-east, some realistic and some involving the supernatural, were published both before and after the author's death. There is also a long-standing fascination with cats that occurs in many of the later tales. In some, like *Size 12* the Tyneside setting is palpably experienced in the dialect used by the children, though none of the locations are made specific. Though the time-slip fantasy novels such as *The Watch House* and *The Wind-Eye* would be held in high regard if they were all that he had ever produced, it is for his stories of Tyneside at war that Robert Westall deserves the greatest recognition. When interviewed he recalled what happened to him when he first started to think about those days of his youth and talked of "a great surge" of memory that never really left him. To borrow one of his own literary devices, each of his books became like a voyage on the "Resurre" taking him back to the world that once was full of pain, full of fear and full of excitement. It is his skill as a writer that makes us want to be a willing passenger on his voyages of creation.

Seal Story 1979 – (57) is set exclusively on Holy Island and is very much a family story. The author, Kathleen Fidler, tells of Aidan Reid, a nine year old who lives with his mother and father and his grandparents in a red-tiled cottage near Ouse Bay. For generations the Reids have been fishermen and Aidan's father and grandfather still use their small boat to earn money by tending lobster pots and catching mackerel. The great days of the offshore herring fishing are now long gone. Life on the island, which despite its causeway, is cut off from the mainland for eight hours each day, is gradually being invaded by influences from outside. Already Aidan's older sister, Kate, now goes to the big secondary school at Tweedmouth, where he too must travel in a few years time. At the start of the story the young boy is dreading the time that this must happen. He feels perfectly at home on the mysterious island with its wild birds and the sounds of the sea. The stories of his grandmother about the seals and the fish have always fascinated him. To stay at home and be a fisherman like his father and his grandfather is all that he wants.

Into the world of this sensitive boy Kathleen Fidler introduces the harsh real-life issue of seal-culling. It is the time of year that the Norwegian marksmen come over to reduce the seal population of the nearby Farne Islands by shooting the males and the older calves. His father and grandfather explain the sad reasons why this must happen. They point out the dilemma of the people of Seahouses who take tourists out to see the famous seals but who know that the seals make big inroads into the available fish stocks. The grandmother is not convinced by this reasoning but family peace is preserved by each person carefully avoiding arguments on this topic.

Aidan's quiet and secure way of life suddenly suffers two disturbing interruptions. The first is from Tom Watson, a boy at his primary school, who is the antithesis of all that Aidan represents. Tom, the son of a relatively affluent trader, is loud and aggressive and constantly wants to show off his material possessions like his newly acquired transistor radio. He needs to boast and bully and is ready to attack anybody who either stands up to him or ignores him. The radio that he carries becomes a symbol of discord and foolish pride in possession. In contrast the mouth-organ that Aidan receives from his grandfather soon clearly represents the more worthy idea of creating something through your own efforts and talents that is both harmonious and beautiful. A further magical but frightening experience is created by Kathleen Fidler when the mouth-organ proves to be the vital link between Aidan and a young seal cub whose mother has been inadvertently killed. The fear that Aidan feels comes from the responsibility for feeding and protecting the young mammal that he knows he has to take on. It has to be a secret – not only from selfish young bullies like Tom but also from the world of grown-ups who allow seal culls to happen.

The tension is now built up carefully by a description of Aidan's struggle to find food for the cub and by making it clear that in spite of all his efforts the young animal appears doomed to die. In the background hovers the malevolent Tom with his slingshot.

In the end the secret is out and the family intervenes. Together with his grandfather and his sister, Aidan helps the young orphan seal recover its strength and learn the harsh lessons of hunting for its own fish. The book ends with the boy's increased understanding of the inexorable rhythms of nature. The seal has to go out into the world to make its way but it is likely to always return now and then to the place where it was saved and nurtured. Aidan now realises that as he grows up he will have to leave the island but that it will always be the home that he goes back to. The grandmother's old tales of the seal people or the "silkies" all fit into this close identification between people and seals and the nature of their lives that the young boy has now seen for himself.

It is certainly a book for younger readers and the two maps, one of the island of Lindisfarne and the other of the small town, each help to guide us through all stages of the story.

Blue Patch the Smuggler by Edric Pennon – 1948 (58) is another little book about Holy Island. It too belongs in a series of adventures that are designed for early readers in primary school. The previous adventures of Jeremy and Vicky, the cousins at the centre of the story, appear to include one amongst the Piskies in Cornwall.

Before they go on holiday to Northumberland Jeremy and Vicky are primed in advance by their grandfather to be on the look-out for adventures. In particular the old man tells them about the career of Ben Blue Patch the Smuggler and the legend of the Priory Phantom.

For a while, when they arrive at their holiday destination, what happens is relatively mundane. The cousins go shell collecting and spend some time watching the grey seal pups from the Farne Islands. Friendly Captain Vince, who rows them about in his little boat, adds a few more details to the stories that their grandfather has told them. Back in the 18th century this part of the Northumberland coast was notorious for its smugglers and for the revenue men who tried to capture them. It seems that Ben Blue Patch wasn't just famous for the blue patch on his face but for the fact that he actually had blue hair.

It is only on the night of the barbecue that strange things begin to happen and that the reader begins to understand that this is a form of "time-slip" novel where anything can happen and probably will !

The medium for their journey to the past proves to be the man dressed in monk's clothing who suddenly appears in the old priory. One second they are in the twentieth century waiting to eat the food with their families and the next they are amongst a smuggler band and dressed in the appropriate 18th century clothing. The smugglers are busy moving casks of contraband brandy down to the coast of Holy Island and are using donkeys to carry them. In a surprisingly short time the children are accepted as companions on the journey and appear to make friends with some of the rogues.

The brandy itself is to be taken to a secret dump on one of the Farne Islands. Before long the children meet up with the famous Ben Blue Patch himself and it is clear that he is the leader of the criminals. As well as his blue hair he is also remarkable for his terrific size and strength. He gives a good demonstration of this when he sinks a revenue boat that is pursuing them by throwing a barrel of brandy from a cliff top so that it smashes through the bottom-boards of the unfortunate vessel. Even whilst the officers of the law are firing their pistols at him Blue Patch remains bold and defiant. Strangely enough, this violent and lawless man appears to accept the children because they are "brave and polite".

Having fought off the forces of law and order on the previous occasion it comes as quite a surprise when the bold smuggler decides to meekly accept surrender when the next encounter comes. Before he is whisked away to face justice Vicky persuades him into giving her a lock of hair as a souvenir before she and Jeremy are swept back into the twentieth century by the reappearance of the Priory Phantom.

The biggest cliché of all is to end a story by having the central characters wonder if it was all a dream. However, by this point in the tale, the young reader will surely have realised that there are no rules of reality in this account – other than it mustn't be too frightening and that the forces of good must triumph over the forces of evil. Blue Patch may be a wild, violent and criminal man but he is kind to children. The revenue officers may be spoil-sports but they are on the side of right and so none of them are killed by Blue Patch's attacks – they merely get soaked when their boat sinks. Even the Priory Phantom, it is strongly hinted, is either Jeremy or Vicky's dad dressed up in an old robe. The young reader can thus have the thrill of meeting someone who is "more like beast than man" whilst remaining safely happy that it is all just a story.

The Long Pilgrimage by George Finkle – 1968 (59) is set during the late eighth century when the seven kingdoms of England, each with its blend of peoples as described in his other Durham based historical novel, *The Twilight Kingdom*, face the new threat of the Viking invader. The story is a saga in four books of the journey and homecoming of Sygwald Osricsson. The kingdom of Northumbria is now ruled over by Aethelred the Bloody from his base in Bamburgh. Eighteen year old Sygwald is a thane whose lands lie in Low Fell at Reageshaef (modern-day Gateshead). After refusing to take an insult from the earl Oswy, who deliberately provokes him at a feast, Sygwald loses his self-control and, in a blood mist of temper, throttles his enemy to death. The death of such a powerful man means his killer is left with only two possible choices: exile or death.

Indeed the central two books of the saga are concerned with Sygwald's travels to France, Spain and practically all the countries that border the "middle sea" or Mediterranean. He takes service under Charlemagne, serves a term as a galley slave and makes enough money as a trader to return and play the "blood-ransom" for Oswy if his relatives still demand it. He brings back with him a wife, several trusty friends and a knowledge of the world and fighting tactics that will serve him well in the near future. For his return coincides with one of the most cataclysmic events in all Northumbria's history – the sacking of the holy minster of Lindisfarne by Viking raiders.

This is a theme that is picked up again in *Madatan* by Peter Carter.

In *Madatan* – 1973 (60) we are soon convinced that eighth century Northumbria is a dangerous place to live. Most readers are aware that the Norsemen are constantly just over the horizon ready to swoop from the sea and raid the largely unprotected coasts. What is less commonly written about is the series of civil wars and rebellions that break out amongst the Northumbrian people every time the question of kingship is raised. The men who become monarchs only retain their power by a mixture of cunning and brutality. Such a man is King Aethelred whose name becomes a by-word for ruthlessness. Exposed to both the dangers of conflict within the kingdom and Vikings in the North Sea stand the early Christian settlements such as Lindisfarne and Jarrow, centres of learning and Church power.

Into this fragile world comes Madah, the Celtic captive of the Northmen. His name means "fox" and "Madatan" is "little fox" – a suitable title for one who is going to need all his wits and cunning to survive. His story is one of two journeys – one physical and one spiritual and, for once, the author does not choose the road to ultimate fulfilment that the early part of the book might seem to suggest. Grim irony seems to dog Madah's footsteps, allowing him survival but not contentment. When he is thrown up by the sea onto the north Northumberland coast after a lucky storm wrecks the Viking fleet he is saved from death by the cross he wears around his neck. Adopted by the church, he uses his talents for languages and also acquires the skills of reading and writing. A life of purposeful work and devotion seems to lie in front of him as he embraces the chance to use his special gifts in what seems a noble service. He even finds a spiritually uplifting reward from carrying out the duties of a local priest in preaching to poor country people.

Just as everything seems settled into a safe pattern Madah finds himself suddenly overwhelmed by two feelings for which he has no answer. The first is the attraction that he feels to one particular young woman; the second is the hatred borne towards him by a powerful enemy. Worst of all, however, is the revelation that the Church that has come to be the centre of his life is just as politically motivated and corruptly devious as the kings and noblemen who rule the country. Having been used and betrayed by the priests and bishops, he leaves behind their world and becomes a wolfshead outlaw. With no standards of conduct to uphold his behaviour deteriorates until it becomes the mere animal instinct for survival. Some of these feelings are purged by an encounter with a hermit but the end of the book leaves the future uncertain.

Most of the terrain of this book is familiar and the reader is taken on journeys to well-known places such as Lindisfarne, Hexham Abbey and York. There is even an eye-witness account of the aftermath to the celebrated Viking raid on Lindisfarne in 793. However, it is the uncompromising picture of the early days of Christianity in this region that brings the biggest surprise and which gives the book its unique flavour.

Another Aeroplane Writer

At the junction of a lonely sunken road and a derelict narrow gauge railway line lies an old shed made out of railway sleepers. Its location is somewhere in the north-east of England and in this unlikely place meet up two of the most famous characters in all of British children's literature. The first of these is Biggles, or Major James Bigglesworth MC, a former officer in the RFC, the hero of over 96 flying adventure books by Captain W.E.Johns, and the second is Ginger Hebblethwaite who becomes first of all his protegé and later a vital member of his team during Biggles' days as squadron leader in the Second World War and his subsequent career in the Special Air Police.

When we first meet him in *Biggles and the Black Peril* – 1935 (61) Ginger is dressed in rags, filthy dirty and making his way slowly across the countryside with the ultimate aim of reaching London to join the R.A.F. He is only fifteen or sixteen years of age, the son of a miner from Smettleworth, and clearly used to living off the land by both honest and dishonest means. Indeed, on the night that Biggles first encounters him he is cooking an impromptu meal the bare bones of which have been supplemented by an illicit egg.

The details of Ginger's early life, as retailed to us by Johns in snippets in different books, are both sparse and enigmatic. In at least two or three of the later books, including the very last completed Biggles adventure, *Biggles Sees Too Much,* Johns has his character declare that he is a Yorkshireman. Yet, if we follow the logic of Johns' geography in *Biggles and the Black Peril,* Ginger has been travelling from his home towards London and passed through Newcastle some few days earlier. This and other details would appear to place the meeting with Biggles somewhere in County Durham, not far from the coast. However, later in the same book Biggles declares that the big house where he was held near to where he first met Ginger was in Northumberland. And so, almost by default, this series story creeps into our north of the Tyne stories. It appears that W.E. Johns was also having trouble remembering the true location of the home of this vital character ! This was in spite of the author having spent a year working in the R.A.F. recruiting office in Newcastle. Other things about Ginger are also destined to remain forever a mystery as well. For instance, Biggles calls him "Ginger" as soon as he sees him and the name sticks so well that we never do learn his real Christian name. In the opening book he is called "Habblethwaite" but this is later modified to Hebblethwaite. All these things, however, are trivial compared to the part that he plays in the first adventure and then in the rest of the massive and massively popular Biggles saga.

The first of the "Biggles" stories were written at the beginning of the 1930s and, surprising at it may seem to us today, they were written for adults. Biggles and his cousin and comrade Algy are pilots in the RFC who survive a series of adventures which are based on the exploits and mishaps of the real pilots of the First World War. However, by the mid 1930s the war was a long way in the past and the Biggles stories needed a transfusion of new ideas if they were to appeal to the young people who had become increasingly "air-minded". Two post-war set adventures: the short stories of *Biggles Flies Again* and the adventure novel *The Cruise of the Condor* had proved Johns could capture the younger market. *Biggles and the Black Peril* and the introduction of Ginger were part of a cunning move to both cement his current market and push towards broadening his appeal.

The essence of the Ginger character is threefold. Firstly, Ginger is young, appearing almost in the standing of a son to Biggles and a younger brother to Algy. He is essentially the reader's point of view. The courage and resourcefulness of Biggles and Algy can now be taken for granted and the reader can both experience the thrills and fears of Ginger as he tries to live up to their awesome reputation. Secondly, he is working class and this counter-balances the public-school educated Biggles and Algy. Thirdly he is northern – whether we accept his own definition as a Yorkshireman or the geographical logic that he is Northumbrian. Factors two and three work strongly in combination with each other. Most of all, he is practical and down to earth. In the early stories he demonstrates the ability to use dodges, ruses and a generally unorthodox approach to all the troubles that confront him. He can scrounge in order to survive and, in the early days, bending or breaking of the law in the interests of justice or survival does not hold any qualms for him. He is a mixture of common-sense, native intelligence and practical skills. In the first three or four adventures he is the one that can carry out the mundane mechanical tasks that keep the 'planes flying. He is not afraid of getting his hands covered in oil and relishes the dirty work that has to be done. Whether Johns was hazy about his northern geography or not, he certainly knew which attributes in Ginger he wanted to bring to his stories. In fact it's all there in this story of the "Black Peril".

For, in the second chapter. Ginger leaps immediately to the aid of the captured Biggles and fearlessly plunges into the adventure without a second thought. The action proceeds at a headlong pace: a car is being used by the enemy – Ginger jabs his knife into the tyre; a dog attacks him as he tries to close in on the house where Biggles is held – Ginger uses the bristles of a broom to drive it away; the enemy needs to be diverted – Ginger starts a small but threatening fire. Little wonder that the rescued Biggles responds appreciatively to the young northern lad who has come to his aid. With his intuitive reading of the lie of the land and his instinctive ability to improvise in the face of danger Ginger could prove invaluable. A few days rest and recuperation at Cramlington aerodrome allows Biggles and Algy to decide Ginger's future. Kitted out with a new suit purchased in Newcastle, he flies south with them to learn how to become a pilot and to worm his way into their latest adventure. By the end of the book Johns has provided his readers with an exciting and interesting juvenile point of view, allowing them to share the exploits of a well-known hero through the eyes of his youngest and most down-to-earth comrade. Even Ginger's language, culled from American gangster films, gives the stories an unexpected vitality and informality as it rubs shoulders with the by now rather antiquated RFC and public school expressions of Biggles and Algy.

Series literature is different and a series of such an extraordinary length as the "Biggles" one, spanning as it does stories set in 1910 *(The Boy Biggles)* to the late 1960s, must allow for some developments in character. For a long time Ginger's youth and vulnerability are constantly used to exploit the horror of some of the situations that the team find themselves in. The outbreak of the Second World War makes Ginger just the right age to serve in a Spitfire squadron and bring home to the youth of the nation just what it means to be "blooded" as one of the famous "few". Even more remarkably the boy from the pit village is allowed a brief romance with an attractive girl from Monaco *(Biggles Fails to Return)*. A warning from his readers apparently convinced W.E.Johns that he couldn't allow

The Castle on Lindisfarne which plays a prominent part in "The Five Shilling Holiday" by Lorna Hill.

Jacket illustration by Victor Ambrus for "Madatan" (OUP 1974), reprinted by permission of Oxford University Press.

A book for younger children about Holy Island and the Farnes.

An exciting 1930s flying adventure that begins in Alnmouth – the birthplace of George E. Rochester.

his hero to "go soft" and the following adventures revert for a while to the pattern of the boy who can't be allowed to grow up. As mentioned above, in the last completed "Biggles" book Ginger declares again that he is a Yorkshireman. However, the long years of service in the Air Police appear to have taken their toll and the irrepressible urchin from the north-east seems to have vanished. A more sober and responsible Ginger has taken his place. However, it should never be forgotten that one of the most vital components of the one of the most popular children's series of all time has its origins in a little shed built of railway sleepers somewhere in the north-east.

At this point it is time we remembered one other Holy Island story which we mentioned in Stage 1 of this guide. That is Aidan Chambers' **Marle** (17) which contrasted life in the city with life on the island in the 1960s. It is hardly surprising that Lorna Hill also wrote a story about this ideal location for adventures. In *The Five Shilling Holiday* – 1995 (62) the children from the "Patience" series of stories have a succession of minor adventures involving both the castle and the causeway.

One other story concerning this stretch of country is worthy of note. This is *The Candlemass Treasure* by Philip Turner – 1988 (63) which takes its account of a modern treasure hunt from the fictional Minster St. Peter in Lincolnshire to the very real Holy Island. Although it deals very effectively with the theme of racism in modern Britain and to a lesser extent with bereavement, it is essentially a puzzle story with cryptic clues to be solved so that the children in the tale can get to the treasure before their very formidable enemy. Maps are provided of both locations and the reader can retrace the steps of the searchers without too much difficulty.

It is a more evasive kingdom that Julian Atterton tries to pin down in *The Last Harper* – 1983 (64), in which he tells the story of Gwion, son of Talhearn the harper, who has always lived in the Celtic settlement of Bryneich which included Caer Brighid (Yeavering Bell), Dun Guayrdi (Bamburgh) and the Isle of Metcaud (Lindisfarne). Raiders from the sea are gradually eroding this territory as the farmers and fishermen of the coastal plain and nearby hills are no match for the savagery of the warriors from the east. One final battle takes away both Gwion's king and his father and all he has left are the traditional songs of the harper. With his injured uncle Gwion he begins the long ride to the kingdom of Rheged, which occupies much of the present-day Lake District and with its capital in Caer Lugualid (Carlisle).

Years pass before Gwion is to see his homeland again, when he returns travelling with a cobbled-together Celtic force, who hope to reoccupy Bamburgh and drive the invaders back into the sea. After a first successful attack they are doomed to ultimate failure. It is a historical irony that the heathen invaders are able to survive because they can retreat and regroup on Lindisfarne, later to be the centre of northern Christianity. Selfishness, pride and treachery cause the Celtic alliance to fall to pieces so that both Gwion and the readers know that the Sea Wolves must win in the end. All that will be left of what once was will be a few place names and the songs that the harpers sing.

The Isle of Mystery – 1951 (65) by Percy F. Westerman is an entirely different sort of story and purports to being nearly wholly set in the north-east of England. As a description unfolds of what is in this story of holiday adventure you will see the reason for the cautious choice of words. However, whatever the reservations one may have about the locale, it is important to recognise that this story is a classic representative of the boys' holiday adventure story that started in the 1920s and reached its heyday in the 1940s and 1950s. Publishers like Blackie, Nelson, Collins and Warnes were churning them out in their thousands. Some of them were very good indeed and some were dreadful. The ingredients were fairly typical – including teenage boys on camping holidays in remote parts of the country, stumbling across adventures involving smugglers, mad inventors and mysterious but definitely untrustworthy foreigners. "By luck and by pluck" – incidentally this is a title of another Westerman adventure – the boys win through in the end. Some authors included females in the storyline but Westerman rarely permitted his heroes mothers never mind companions or, whisper it quietly, girlfriends. There are many excellent stories in this mould and writers proved remarkably adaptable at weaving plots that enthralled their readers whilst satisfying the formula, including a set number of pages, enforced by the publishers. Unfortunately, *The Isle of Mystery* is not one of Westerman's best efforts, though once or twice descriptions of individual stretches of action reveal what he could do when he marshalled all his resources.

Study the map of the coast near the town of Berwick and you will look in vain for an island called Black Scar which resembles the Rock of Gibraltar and which is connected to the mainland by a causeway which is covered at high tide. In effect Westerman has taken some of the features of Bass Rock and blended them with the idea of Holy Island. This is the venue for the holiday adventure of three boys from a technical college in the south of England. The alleged main purpose of their holiday is bird-watching but any reader of this type of story knows that they are really there to get themselves into trouble. Fortunately one end of the island of Black Scar is occupied by a suitably mad scientist who is apparently constructing a rocket to go to the moon. His behaviour is appropriately quixotic so that one moment he is helping one of the boys escape from a dramatic cliff accident and the next he is standing there literally foaming at the mouth. The agent for the man who owns the island (he's an "agent" when south of the border and a "factor" when to the north) cheerfully calls him "yon loon, Dellifer." After the British foreign secretary, staying at the local mainland hotel to enjoy a golfing holiday on the nearby links, is kidnapped and taken out to a mystery submarine, the story proceeds along its usual lines. A mysterious and enormous stranger lands on the island after swimming in from the North Sea. He claims to be Turkish but in fact belongs to the International Brotherhood of Democratic Freedom. He got washed overboard from the submarine when it dived rather too quickly. Just when it seems the story can't get any sillier it turns out that Dellifer isn't really aiming his rocket at the moon but is sending a devastating bomb to Vorofgrad, the city which is the headquarters of the mysterious organisation.

From this summary of about half the plot you can see that the whole storyline is rather preposterous. Westerman's vision of this part of the north-east is also rather hit and miss in its identification of typical features and really quite sloppy in the consistency with which it deals with local geography. Thus, having started the book with Berwick as the nearest port, Westerman later refers to Blyth as the most adjacent harbour. There are also references to fetching the police from the nearest police station in Morpeth. Two supposedly local characters, a fisherman and his red-headed son, are shown to be enterprising and helpful. They are also given what might be described as a semblance of a northern accent with the ubiquitous "Ah" replacing "I" as required every time it appears in the dialogue. The contrast between these deferential Northumbrians and the "old chaps" and "old boys" as the three young heroes talk amongst themselves makes for quaint reading nowadays.

Without doubt Percy F. Westerman's natural home in the world of literature was in amongst the sailing vessels and small cargo tramps that plied the seas in the first half of the twentieth century. However, it must be admitted that when be brought his readers ashore to his fictional Northumberland what he describes is no more convincing than his invention of the town of Vorofgrad and its International Brotherhood of Democratic Freedom.

And so, after our long trek down the river and up the coast, we have reached Berwick-upon-Tweed and the nearby Scottish border. It is a town we shall arrive in again as we follow the trail of Alys and her companion on their quest to Scotland in *Ransom for a Knight*, but that is only after we have followed their journey to deepest Northumberland in the final quarter of this book.

To Hexham and the Roman Wall

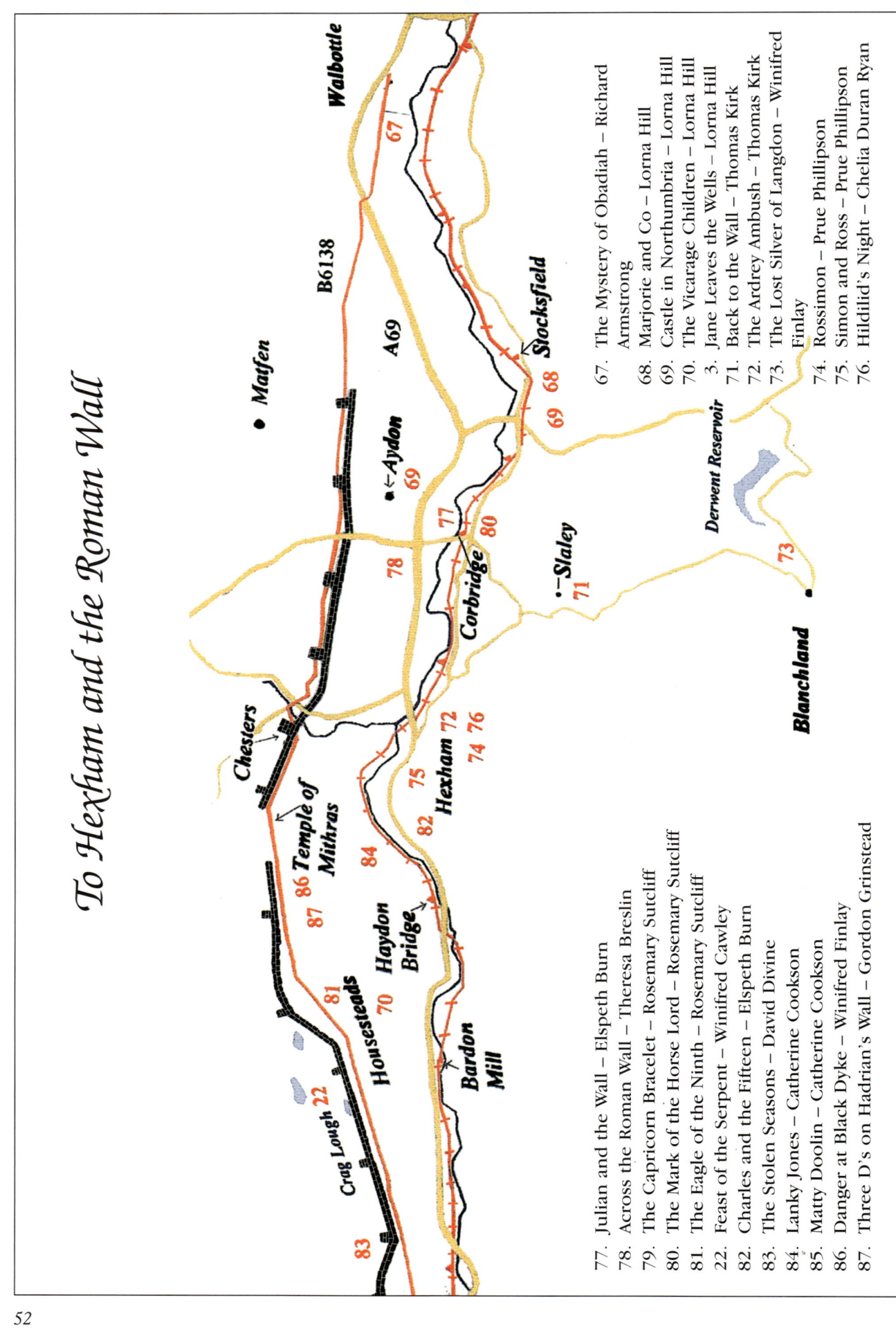

77. Julian and the Wall – Elspeth Burn
78. Across the Roman Wall – Theresa Breslin
79. The Capricorn Bracelet – Rosemary Sutcliff
80. The Mark of the Horse Lord – Rosemary Sutcliff
81. The Eagle of the Ninth – Rosemary Sutcliff
22. Feast of the Serpent – Winifred Cawley
82. Charles and the Fifteen – Elspeth Burn
83. The Stolen Seasons – David Divine
84. Lanky Jones – Catherine Cookson
85. Matty Doolin – Catherine Cookson
86. Danger at Black Dyke – Winifred Finlay
87. Three D's on Hadrian's Wall – Gordon Grinstead

67. The Mystery of Obadiah – Richard Armstrong
68. Marjorie and Co – Lorna Hill
69. Castle in Northumbria – Lorna Hill
70. The Vicarage Children – Lorna Hill
3. Jane Leaves the Wells – Lorna Hill
71. Back to the Wall – Thomas Kirk
72. The Ardrey Ambush – Thomas Kirk
73. The Lost Silver of Langdon – Winifred Finlay
74. Rossimon – Prue Phillipson
75. Simon and Ross – Prue Phillipson
76. Hildilid's Night – Chelia Duran Ryan

52

Danger at Black Dyke – The lone hiker is about to encounter the Men of Mithras.

Stage 3: To Hexham and the Roman Wall

A MAP of the main part of the Tyne Valley shows us that there are three ways of exploring towards the west. Firstly there is the Newcastle to Carlisle railway with stations placed at regular intervals, quite often at significant places in the children's stories that are set in this part of the county. However, there is little doubt that exploring by car or tourist bus is by far the best option. South of the river the A695 wends its way through Blaydon and Prudhoe and Stocksfield until eventually it reaches the outskirts of the market town of Hexham. North of the river the trunk road, the A69, is by far the fastest way of reaching the main towns that lie along the valley bottom. Quite early on there is an opportunity to avoid the headlong rush by taking the turn-off for Walbottle and following the B6528 to Heddon-on-the-Wall. A right turn on to the B6318 and you cross above the frenetic A69 and you are on the famous Military Road built along the line of the Wall itself. Thus eventually the Roman Wall is lying on your left to the south and then at Chollerford you cross until the road continues to run parallel, but this time with the most striking visions of the ruins to the north.

The literary journey really starts just after you leave Newcastle, with the district around Walbottle and Newburn where Richard Armstrong was born and spent the early years of his life.

Walbottle

The Mystery of Obadiah – (67) is the third and perhaps least important of Richard Armstrong's books to be set in the north-east. Chronologically, however, it comes first, being published in 1943. It is simply a boy's adventure story set somewhere in the Tyne Valley with the fells to the north. Thias, the hero of *Sabotage at the Forge* is here only thirteen but already showing the leadership qualities that mark him out in the later book. With his two friends he sets out to find the perpetrator of a series of local burglaries. A few sketches of village life are combined with a story where the villain has his den in old mine workings which are eventually explored by the boys. Already Armstrong is interested in the essence of team-work and leadership qualities. Lost underground, the boys work out their own salvation as much by careful rational thought as by courage and resolution.

A study of Richard Armstrong's own life and of his later work reveals in so many ways that he was just like his juvenile hero, Thias. The recurring theme of a young man taking responsibility and thus "finding himself" continues in each of Armstrong's sea-going stories such as *Danger Rock* and *Sea Change*. For the author took Thias' route to fulfilment as an officer in the merchant navy but later, and more importantly for us, he also discovered the skills within himself to become a superb storyteller and to record those important ways of life in pit villages and large foundries that are gone forever.

Lorna's World – Stocksfield, Matfen, Aydon, Bellingham, the Wall

No matter where we travel in Northumberland we will meet with the stories of Lorna Hill. A casual reader of a few tales might not realise that all thirty-three books are very carefully inter-connected, with major characters in one series playing cameo roles in another. However, in one way of thinking, the stories really all start in Matfen and Stocksfield. For Matfen is where Lorna was the wife of the local vicar and where in the freezing cold vicarage she would sit down late at night to write the first adventures in school exercise books as birthday and Christmas presents for her daughter Vicki. The very first story **Marjorie & Co** – 1948 (68) is set amongst the wealthy middle-class families of Stocksfield where Vicki went to school just before the Second World War with her friend who in the books was disguised under the name of Marjorie.

Without doubt the main concern of each of the "Marjorie" books is the developing relationships between the four central characters and the additional delight comes from the way in which all the action is played out against a back-drop of different parts of the Northumbrian countryside. Though all of the children come from exclusively middle-class homes and though they all attend public schools in different parts of Britain, there is a universality in their behaviour that makes the idea of "class" irrelevant. The characters are clear and distinct but very far from being stereotypical. The books are full of comedy, pathos, drama and painful self-reflection. The first surprise is that Marjorie is certainly not the heroine of the series – if anything she is the villain. She is wilful, selfish, thoughtless, lacking in patience and, at times, wantonly cruel. Thus she is doubly fascinating to read about. When we discover that she is also beautiful, full of life and determination and misguided courage, it is easy to understand why she is never finally and irrevocably expelled from the "clan" that the children form themselves into.

On the other side of the moral divide is Guy Charlton, the acknowledged leader of the clan, and the senior member at the age of sixteen. Guy's leadership and Marjorie's straying from the paths of righteous behaviour are the underlying plots in each of the books. At times Guy is so frustratingly right that you want him to fail, and when he blunders in his treatment of the girls you are drawn to him more because of his mistakes than because of his god-like "rightness" on other occasions. Guy is a boy of both physical and moral courage and he has very clear ideas about behaviour that stand in the face of the fads of fashion that appear so attractive to teenage girls. Guy is accomplished at everything he attempts and he is cheerfully patient in the way in which tries to show the others the right and wrong methods of doing things. His Achilles heel, if he really has one, is the feeling of protectiveness he feels towards Esmé, the most outwardly sensitive and the youngest of the three girls in the clan. Esmé's kindness extends to all of the animal kingdom, including those creatures that other people might consider to be pests. This makes her particularly vulnerable to some of the scenes that they come across in the course of their explorations of the countryside.

The final girl in the group is Pansy Pierce, aged fourteen like the others, but with a different set of problems to face as she grows up. It is through her that Lorna Hill chooses to tell each of the stories in the first person. Indeed it would be fair to say that Pan's perspective is one of the main reasons why the stories work so well and give such an impression of emotional depth that other writers of children's stories find so hard to achieve. Marjorie, Guy and Esmé are all very open characters whose thoughts and feelings are on the surface and easily recorded by Pan. Pan herself, however, is less confident, totally convinced of her own plainness in comparison to Marjorie and Esmé, less accomplished as a rider and full of strange longings and fears.

The role of fifth member of the clan is sometimes taken by Peter and sometimes by Toby, the youngest of the boys, who suffers from an over-protective mother. However, both boys play minor parts and they are completely overshadowed by Guy and his disputes with Marjorie. His attempts to control her conduct mostly meet with our approval. However, there is a zest in her wickedness that makes her an anti-heroine who the stories can't do without. The moment in **Castle in Northumbria** (69) when she picks up the bread knife and slashes at a white dress that has been sent to her, so that it can't be borrowed by another girl for a May pageant, is both thrilling and appalling. Much worse in *Stolen Holiday* is the way Marjorie scratches Esmé's face when not chosen as Harvest Queen and her jealousy overcomes her completely. In spite of all

The Stolen Seasons – An archaeological dig turns into a nightmare chase.

punishments, including a beating on the backside with a sand-shoe by Guy, Marjorie proves satisfyingly incorrigible.

At first sight it might be possible to mistake both the "Marjorie" and "Patience" stories as mere pony stories set in Northumberland. However, in spite of their sojourns in border peels, border castles and in bungalows amongst the sand dunes near Beadnell, there is no sense of romantic escape. Pan may dream of the border raiders clattering over the cobblestones of the castle in Northumbria but she is careful to record just how difficult it is to get the mud off your clothes once you have pulled a mucky sheep out of a mire. Marjorie may have the conventional dramatic cliff accident on the Farne Islands in *Stolen Holiday* but Lorna Hill actually creates a deeper feeling of emotional upset by her description of the way in which Guy carries Esmé away from the cornfield near Bamburgh as the last pieces of the crop are cut down and the boys and men begin the savage slaughter of the trapped animals. There is also the careful record of the mundane details of acquiring food and keeping themselves clean. However, the main pre-occupation of each story is the never-ending battle of wills between Guy and Marjorie and the collateral effect on the other members of the clan. That these battles take place in vividly but briefly described scenery is an added bonus.

The "Patience" series introduces us to another set of children whose holiday adventures are followed in the Northumberland countryside. Much of the territory that is described overlaps with that of the "Guy and Marjorie" clan. Indeed the leading male character, David Elliott, is a cousin of Guy Charlton and appears briefly in *Border Peel* where Guy won the saddle in the gymkhana with David in second place. The emotional tensions in this series are different and this time "Patience", though the youngest of the five children, is clearly meant to be a girl whom we can like and admire. She is both spirited and affectionate and totally devoted to her brother, David, whom she worships like a god. In return David is protective and the person he needs to protect her from is their father. The anger and malevolence of Colonel Elliott are well recognised by each of the children. The narrator of this set of "Patience" stories is Judy and there is enough difference between her and the Pansy Pierce character for the reader to appreciate a whole new identity as revealed from the inside.

The stories in each series move from the "tame" countryside around Stocksfield and the Tyne Valley to exciting camps and the life in big houses up on the moors around Bellingham. Thus the writer's imagination takes the real Aydon Castle from near Corbridge and moves it a satisfying 30 miles or so north-westwards out into the real Northumberland. It really would take a life-time of Sherlock Holmes deduction to work out just which local castle, peel house, peel tower or bastle she "borrowed" for the many families that she placed in and around the triangle formed by the confluence of the A696 and the A68. I am privileged enough to have a copy of the original map with its little crosses that she used to mark the different houses that she invented to fit on to the minor roads that surround Bellingham and Hesleyside. It's all very evasive territory. You can suspect that Chipchase Castle near Wark was the model for the home of the obnoxious Sir Nigel Monkhouse but you can't be sure. On the other hand the vicarage at Staneshaw that was the model for the home of the family in *The Vicarage Children* – 1961 (70) trilogy is clearly a mixture of where Lorna lived in Matfen and the more interesting house of some friends near the Roman Wall. Nowadays few visitors to the museum at Vindolanda will realise that the building they are standing in (called Chesterholm) is in fact where a local author described the teenage years of Allison and Mandy !

It would be a fruitless exercise to attempt to track in this account all the places and incidents of the fourteen books in the "Wells" series. However, it is important to understand the way in which Lorna Hill moves her consideration of her home area into the different world of the young romance novel. The first five stories are the strongest; the remainder have many interesting scenes but are prone to repetition and do not have the same sustained intensity of feeling. However, because we are dealing with the phenomenon of series literature the gradual falling off in quality matters very little. This is because the characters have become old friends, with some of the early heroes and heroines melting into the background as they grow older but still exercising either a benevolent or malevolent presence over the main protagonists of the later books. In fact, by the time of the last few books, the reader is well into the second generation and Veronica, who was the down-trodden young ballerina in *A Dream of Sadler's Wells,* has become *prima ballerina assoluta,* a powerful figure in the world of ballet and the mother of Vicki who has her own story of losing and finding love to be told. Present all the way through the series are the views of Northumbrian life and countryside, exciting journeys through the worst of weathers and interesting glimpses of areas of the city of Newcastle. In the best of the stories the landscapes and townscapes are transformed from being mere stages for the action and become the means by which Lorna Hill informs us of character and behaviour. Quite often, without effort and almost imperceptibly, the settings take on a symbolic importance that only becomes apparent upon close study. This is best illustrated by a brief look at *Jane Leaves the Wells* (3B – see page 11 for 3A), the fifth and perhaps the most important book in the series.

Jane is a young ballerina who is in the process of breaking through to the top rank of her profession. Mariella, her cousin, has rejected the world of her mother, a world-renowned ballerina, and opted for life in the Northumberland countryside. Throughout the book Lorna Hill draws an elaborate contrast between the world of art and the world of nature. In order to succeed, Jane has to enter a world of make-believe and of rigid discipline. On the other hand Mariella is captivated by the sights and sounds of the rugged countryside that she has grown to love. Unfortunately she also believes herself to be in love with Nigel, an extremely handsome but very selfish and sometimes cruel young man – the ultimate "huntin', fishin', shootin'" villain. The contrasting positions of the two girls are conveyed by an arresting passage about the way in which the garden of the village school teacher has suddenly been brought under order and control. There is now a consistent formality about the garden, for it possesses the same rigid lines and control that are so essential to some aspects of ballet. Mariella had preferred it in all its riotous spontaneity, its natural beauty. She is a gifted rider and takes to all the country pursuits with enthusiasm and understanding. Jane was force-fed horse-riding from a very early age and found she had neither the aptitude nor the enthusiasm for horses and all that goes with it. The behaviour of the bullying Nigel merely confirmed how much she loathed anything to do with horses. Only her courage when a child in rescuing a sheep near Housesteads on Hadrian's Wall convinces him and her own family that she is worth anything at all. Thus, when she finds fulfilment and success in the world of ballet, she discovers a spirit within herself that makes her challenge the conventions of the world in which she has grown up. Yet, like Mariella, she too risks being taken in by the surface appearance of things for she has proved susceptible to the charms of her dancing partner, the shallow and vain Josef. The catalyst for converting all these ingredients into a happy ending is contained in the character that Lorna Hill believes enshrines all that is best about the north-east of England and that is Guy Charlton, the central juvenile lead from both the "Marjorie" and "Patience" books. His courtship of Jane is set against her sudden success in the world of ballet. He is kind, considerate, self-denying and yet still firmly determined and forthright in his behaviour. The values of art are set against the values of life and love in the Northumberland countryside. With his tender and skilful approach Guy even enables Jane to overcome her childhood fear and loathing of horses and she becomes a "Northumbrian" again. When Jane finally chooses him whilst at the height of her fame, Guy tells her in his telegram not to think of it as leaving the Wells but as finally coming "home".

In the first few "Wells" books the counterpoint to the story of Guy and Jane has been the stormy romance of Veronica and Sebastian. Here the supreme achievements of the ballet dancer and the composer are shown to be partly derived from the inspiration that the Northumbrian countryside has given them. Lorna Hill suggests that they can create beautiful art partly because they have lived amongst the beauties of the Northumberland countryside. Their temperaments are different and they have discovered a different kind of "truth". On a more mundane and human level, even Mariella eventually learns that the outer signs of looking like a Greek god cannot conceal Nigel's shallow and selfish character. The presiding theme of the series is Lorna Hill's idea that generosity of spirit, selflessness and concern for others brings both success in the world of art and happiness in one's private life. It is, in essence, a Christian message. A part of the tension of the series is derived from the different ways in which she shows her heroines struggling to succeed in the world of dance whilst simultaneously gaining knowledge about the young men who offer themselves as potential partners. As one might expect from the author who created "Marjorie", there are also some wonderful villains. Veronica's cousin, Fiona, is diabolically cruel to her in the very first story, *A Dream of Sadler's Wells* and Nigel, after losing Mariella, begins to inflict his odious personality on poor Sylvia Swan, masking his true nature once again under a suave and handsome exterior. The self-centred nature of Fiona and Nigel extends throughout most of the books in the series and we follow their fates with almost as much interest as those of the heroines and heroes.

Some of the values, some of the class assumptions, and some of the fashions, which were an integral part of her world, may now have passed away. However, a revisit to the best books of this author will demonstrate that her principles were sound and that she had lots to say about friendship and love that still rings true in the changed world of the new millennium.

Exploring the possibilities of Stocksfield, Matfen and Aydon Castle can now be followed by an excursion to the south before we press on to Corbridge and Hexham.

Slaley and Blanchland

There are three books by Thomas Kirk about the Robinson family who live in a clearing in a forest near Slaley Hall. However, only the first of these, **Back to the Wall** – 1967 (71) deals in any detail with events in the north-east of England.

The real flavour of the rest of the book is given to the reader as soon as this story starts, for the author has provided a plot which depends upon a series of chases to and from different locations in the region, mostly in the Tyne Valley. The second half of the plot allows a lapse of time from the Christmas to the Easter holidays. The criminals in the story are waiting for the "heat" to die down so that they can divide the proceeds of their robbery. Unfortunately for them a cryptogram which the boss has drawn up to organise the share-out meeting has fallen into the hands of both the police and the children. Between Christmas and Easter the two Robinson children puzzle it all out. There are tantalising references to local landmarks, to train times and to letters of the alphabet which seem to stand for the members of the gang. The author presents this to the reader to solve as well.

Later the author supplements his narrative by neat drawings of important locations as the story builds to a climax. Thus we have a sketch of the platforms of Bardon Mill station, another one of the paths leading from the inn at Twice Brewed to the Roman Wall and finally one of the Staward Bridge and the River Allen. The book ends with a car chase and the author ensures that you can trace every mile of the way by the meticulous detail of his narrative.

This is an adventure story which depends upon one ingredient above all others and that is pace. Nothing irrelevant or everyday is allowed to delay the action. Even a potentially mundane and quiet scene such as when William goes for a haircut in Hexham turns into a frantic hunt for a mysterious limping stranger. As a consequence of this sort of frenetic claustrophobia the development of character and relationships is reduced to a series of snapshots, though the affectionate bantering between brother and sister and their parents provides enough hints about their personalities for the reader to share their fears and thrills. The behaviour of the villains is less well sustained and the rationale for why they are in the north-east and why they organised their activities in this way would probably not stand up to a robust examination. However, the author makes sure you never pause for deeper thought. Even the landscapes seem only to be there to be the place where things can happen and happen quickly. However, all these features would be in total accordance with the aim of providing children with a nearly grown-up action thriller.

Other William and Susan Robinson stories in the series take the children to Lincolnshire and to southern Ireland. In one, ***The Ardrey Ambush*** – 1969 (72) the action begins in

Blanchland – The quest for "The Lost Silver of Langdon" begins in this sleepy village.

Hexham courthouse and later there is a description of the family making its way across country to Stranraer to catch the ferry.

The Lost Silver of Langdon – 1955 (73) by Winifred Finlay is another story of Ricky, Paul and Judith whom we can meet again in *Castle for Four* and *Storm Over Cheviot*. It begins with a wonderfully atmospheric scene in Blanchland and a description of the Lord Crewe Arms but then, tantalisingly from the point of view of the restrictions of this book, crosses the border into County Durham for the main part of the story. A small part of the tension in the tale is provided by Judith's anxious wait for her 'A' level results from her school in Newcastle.

Hexham

The nature of friendship and the demands of individuality are two themes in *Rossimon* – 1997 (74) and its sequel *Simon and Ross* – 1998 (75) by Prue Phillipson. Ross Winterton is the new boy in class 7W at the middle school in Brynford. Everything about him is the complete opposite to the nature of the boy whom he chooses for his friend: Simon Tree, the son of a man who works in the local tailor's shop. Ross is loud, aggressive and confident, seemingly able to deal effortlessly with every situation that arises, from taking tea with the Tree family to seeing off the school bully. Simon is the youngest of a large family with three elder sisters and, somewhere in the process of growing to the age of eleven, he has struggled to find any inner confidence. To be chosen by Ross as his closest friend seems unbelievably wonderful and begins the transformation of his life. Unhappily not all the changes are for the good. On the one hand, with Ross by his side, Simon is encouraged into joining the Abbey choir and into going for an audition for the school musical, "Oliver". However, on the other, he finds himself drawn into a web of lies and half-truths that are totally at odds with Simon's gentle Christian upbringing.

Whilst Simon is being taken out of himself by Ross' irreverent and dynamic personality, the two sets of parents are meeting crises in their lives in radically different ways. Ross' parents, struggling to establish a consultancy business in the small market town, are at constant war with each other and Simon is appalled to witness Ross being beaten by his father. Simon's own father is being made redundant as the small tailor's shop is to be sold and then closed down. The world of big business as represented by the arrival of the Supacentre is changing the face of the world that he has known. The old-fashioned but strong family values of the Tree family are contrasted with the wild and almost Bohemian behaviour of the Winterton parents.

The fusion of the two boys in the joint personality of Rossimon and its consequences for the apparently weaker member of the pairing, Simon, is particularly gripping in its intensity and the end of the adventure is not at all predictable. Though she has given Hexham the fictional name of Brynford, Prue Phillipson, has created a very clear picture of the town and its surroundings. Simon's feeling for the Abbey and the services that take place there are particularly moving. When his father becomes the verger, after the death of the previous incumbent, it seems to the rest of the family that God has given a sign that their lives, temporarily blighted by the redundancy, are going to improve for the better. The way in which the older girls in the Tree family come home for the weekend and witness Simon's debut in the choir and the installation of their father in his new role creates a genuine feeling of a close-knit small town life with its habitual rituals and pleasures.

Because Ross is an outsider, because he is without principles and because he appears to receive little emotional nourishment at home, he is both exciting to Simon

Hexham Abbey – The thinly disguised abbey at the centre of "Rossimon".

and uncomfortable for the reader to cope with. He is both "flash" and fragile, an entirely unsuitable companion for the sensitive and vulnerable Simon. This is exemplified by the visit that the two boys make to the Supacentre (surely the MetroCentre) and Ross spends his money with reckless abandon. Simon ends up both sick and dismayed, knowing that he has yet another secret to keep back inside himself. Other escapades are more exhilarating and reflect more warmly the fun that boys can have when they give full rein to their imaginations. Thus Rossimon builds a den inside the remains of the old railway bridge over the Bryn (the Tyne) near where the north and south Bryn (Tyne) meet. More excitingly, as Rossimon, they fight the school bully and his gang, and Simon discovers his courage and realises that he no longer dreads going to school.

Three years after the dramatic end of *Rossimon* the author takes up the tale of the friendship when Ross gets down from a lorry outside Midcaster (Newcastle) station and catches the small train to Brynford (Hexham) again. *Simon and Ross* deals with the same two boys but this time they are facing their last year at school. The separating of their names in the title emphasises the ways in which the author shows them developing as individuals. Ross has decided to take charge of his own destiny and throw off the lack of care of his semi-alcoholic mother and his ruthless but ultimately feckless father who have now separated. He is determined to finish his schooling at the same establishment as Simon, choosing, of course, the crucial terms in the build-up to the vital GCSEs for this drastic move. Once again his arrival on the scene is to have a dramatic effect on the life of Simon and the rest of his family. In particular, Simon's cousin James is drawn into a web of petty crime and bullying that somehow also captures the other two boys whilst they attempt to rebuild their once close relationship. Other tensions within the Tree family also begin to emerge and the reader learns far more about the youngest of Simon's three sisters, Joanna. The problems of selecting the right direction in your life are shown not to be the exclusive property of teenagers. The author cleverly shows that there is no end-point, no final destination of certain happiness. Even Mr. Tree, who has found his true calling in the job of verger, has to struggle with the troubles and anxieties he has about his own children and the appropriateness of what he has to offer at the local youth club.

A formal inter-school debate about drug-taking forces both Ross and Joanna to confront their attitudes to the Christian belief that is the backbone of the Tree family. In the time of crisis Ross finds that he needs the support of Simon and his old-fashioned stick-in-the-mud father. Many of his customary selfish channels of thought are suddenly but convincingly diverted into new directions. The book ends with Ross having conquered some of the devils that have driven him to becoming a law unto himself, and with him now ready to confront even the new demands of his parents, who have begun to resurrect their collapsed marriage. The attraction that he feels for Joanna, and which she partly reciprocates in spite of the eight year age difference, makes him re-evaluate his whole attitude towards girls. In spite of his intelligence and his glib charm Ross discovers that he still has a lot to learn. His problems are not resolved and the future remains uncertain.

Both books have a lot to offer to young readers for the gradual shading in of the moral landscape is enlivened by dramatic incident, authentic situations and settings, and characters whose troubles and fears they can share.

Hildilid's Night – 1971 (76) by Chelia Duran Ryan is a picture book for young children. The illustrations by Arnold Lobel are in black and white and cover 30 full pages.

Hildilid is an old woman who lives in the hills near Hexham. She has decided that she doesn't like the night and that she is going to find the way to get rid of it. Each of the illustrations then show her trying different methods of expulsion. Some of the methods are violent, including attempts to boil the night and singe the night. Other devices she employs include singing it lullabies and digging a grave for it. From a child's point of view the highlight of the text is when she does the most forbidden thing of all – she spits at the night !

All Hildilid's attempts are to no avail for the night remains. Finally she turns her back on it. This is the instant that the sun rises and the night disappears. Poor Hildilid is so tired that she doesn't realise that it has gone; she is fast asleep in bed. By the time she gets up the night will have returned and the battle can begin all over again.

The Roman Wall – Roman Times

For her two books Elspeth Burn chose subjects which are over fifteen hundred years apart in time but are connected by the small area of countryside around the heart of the Roman Wall. ***Julian and the Wall*** – 1968 (77) is based around incidents in the life of the twelve year old son of the Roman commander of Corstopitum (Corbridge). The story is set in the reign of the Emperor Commodus, sixty years after the completion of Hadrian's Wall. The basic plot is about Julian's involvement in the suppressing of a rebellion by the Caledonian peoples who have not learned to accept the "Pax Romana" and all the material benefits it brings. The desire for freedom runs deep within all of the conquered tribesmen and, from time to time, it causes them to reject the comfort and certainty of organised life and to take on the might of the greatest military regime that the ancient world has ever known. Julian's need to help his father maintain this uneasy status quo has grown partly out of duty to his family but also from his friendship with Neil and his family, a group of Caledonian people to whom he has grown very close. At the very least, he feels that if he can help his father nip the uprising in the bud, then a terrible massacre will be prevented.

Three main incidents make up the whole story. The first is an unexpected expedition with his father north of the wall. Julian glories in the opportunity for hunting in the refreshing and seductively attractive countryside. The second takes Julian along the wall in the direction of Chesters with a repair gang. This gives the author an ideal opportunity to describe the construction of the wall and the duties of soldiers who are detailed to defend it. At this point it is worth mentioning the picture on the dustwrapper of the book which sums up the essence of the story. A kneeling Roman soldier is providing Julian with a platform for him to look out northwards. The countryside lies before him, wild, beautiful and exciting. He gets down from his perch to gaze to the south and here he sees cultivated fields, well-built houses and the all the other marks of civilisation. Elspeth Burn convinces us that both ways of life are worth fighting for but also that peace between the two peoples is worth preserving. Just how Julian manages to help avert a whole-scale uprising and to bring about the unmasking of a traitor is the core of the third section of the book.

Loyalty is a complicated business and Julian's dilemma about the right course of action to take makes for interesting reading. A map at the front of the book guides the reader clearly through each stage of the action.

Across the Roman Wall – 1997 (78) by Theresa Breslin is an 87 page novel in the "Flashbacks" series for younger children. It begins in Corstopitum in the year 397 AD when the Roman Empire, riven by internal dissension, is beginning to lose its grip on some of its overseas provinces, including Britain. To present the gradual slide into the Dark Ages on a more human scale the author chooses two young people as her central characters and examines their linked fortunes in this changing world. Marinetta, the daughter of Cedric the local magistrate, clashes with Lucius Calvus, an arrogant young man in the company of his uncle, Titus Calvus, a senior government official who is collecting information about traitors and the state of hostility of the local tribes. By the end of chapter one Lucius has behaved so badly and she has stood up to him so bravely that each vows that they never want to see each other again. Even the most inexperienced reader knows better and awaits their next encounter with anticipation.

Next comes the raid and their capture by Celtic tribesmen and the beginning of a long journey which reveals just how far the standards of the Roman world have been undermined. Even the sentries at one of the gates on Hadrian's Wall have been bribed to let the raiders go through to the north unchallenged. For both young people all the ideas that have so far been the guiding principles of their lives have to be readjusted. In their time of trial they begin to reach out towards each other.

It is at this point in the narrative that the story becomes both too big and too adult for the format and the age of the readers. Journeys to a slave market in Africa and then onwards to Rome (and back again) are accomplished in seemingly very little time and with little descriptive detail. Marinetta, a young and beautiful girl, is handled by Celtic raiders, sea pirates, an African slave marketeer and spends time as a slave, yet loses no more than her beautiful hair.

The story of Marinetta and Lucius is bound to end happily and the author chooses the same image employed by Rosemary Sutcliff in *The Lantern Bearers* to suggest the future of Britain. Marinetta is determined to pick up her life again in her home town (but this time with Lucius). Nowhere is safe but it is their duty to keep the lamp burning even if there is a dark night ahead of them. The young reader of this book, having been given an interesting introduction, could, with the passage of years, move on to the broader and more detailed canvas of Roman life that is to be found in *The Eagle of the Ninth* and the other Sutcliff Roman novels.

For Rosemary Sutcliff has always been considered amongst the front rank of those novelists writing for children who took historical subjects as the basis for their tales. Her writings on the Roman occupation of Britain lead almost inevitably to a consideration of those people on both sides of the divided nation who lived together for more than four hundred years. The greatest symbol of this division is, of course, the Roman Wall between Wallsend and the Solway Firth, which, for a time, marked the limit of imperial expansion and became truly the "last frontier" of a particular form of civilisation. The heroes of most of Sutcliff's stories become involved in an outward journey to some tangible fulfilment, whilst at the same time coming to terms with something in their own spirit that has pushed them to undertake this quest. Three books by Sutcliff, partly set in this region, explore this strange rootlessness, this mish-mash of allegiances, that makes the reader appreciate both the values and life-style of the native Celtic peoples and the very different systems of behaviour that underlie the world of Rome.

The Capricorn Bracelet – 1973 (79) is a collection of linked short stories, each dealing with a different period in the Roman occupation. At first each story seems to be about how the bracelet of the title is passed on from one generation of a Roman family to the next. Closer consideration makes you realise that in each case, though the name of Lucius Calpurnius may go from father to son, the Roman bloodline is being constantly diluted by marriages to the women of the local tribes. By the end of the occupation, when the last men of Rome sail from Britain never to return, the final Lucianus of the line leaves the now redundant wall and blends into the tribes who now have a new fight on their hands with the Saxon invaders. Before this happens Sutcliff has given us many superb impressions of what life may have been like on the wall itself. She brings out the loneliness and comradeship of the soldiers in their sometimes uncomfortable outposts. She shows us Frontinus, the chief engineer, who has lost his wife in childbirth and who has nothing to lavish his affection on but the wall itself. He progresses from one end to the other, demanding and getting high standards of craftsmanship during the period of its construction. In the end he loses his life in a minor skirmish, trying to prevent a group of horse-trading tribesmen from breaking through one of its weak points. Just as moving is the story in which the novice leader wins the respect and affection of his cavalry troop by defending one of his men on latrine duty who has been caught painting an unflattering portrait of the legate. The mingling of the two peoples is also conveyed in the story in which the Roman soldier leaves the eagles to become the apprentice craftsman to the tribal blacksmith whilst the adopted brother of the blacksmith rides to the wall to take up the service of the "red crests". So-called civilisation and so-called barbarism are thrust alongside each other and Sutcliff encourages you to give your allegiance to neither or to both.

The two full-length stories that concern the Wall and the tribes of northern Britain are ***The Mark of the Horse Lord*** – 1965 (80) and ***The Eagle of the Ninth*** – 1954 (81). In the first of these Sutcliff presents us with a Celtic warrior who was taken as a slave and who has lost touch with all those influences that had shaped the life of his family for generations. Originally a charioteer, Phaedrus was condemned to a life as a gladiator when his master got deeply into debt. The rules of the ring are all that matters in his life where eventual, bloody death seems a certainty and where crippling injury is an everyday hazard. Then arrives the day of Phaedrus' last fight in the arena of Corstopitum. By a miracle he wins the wooden foil, the symbol of his freedom, but at the cost of the death of his only friend, Vortimax, against whom he had been matched in single combat. Freedom, without the discipline of the gladiator school, soon proves meaningless and Rosemary Sutcliff gives a clear picture of how easy it was to get into trouble in the drinking taverns of a frontier town like Corstopitum.

It is only when he reaches his lowest ebb, locked up in the town gaol, that Phaedrus is given a glimpse of his route back to salvation. The rest of the story concerns his impersonation of the tribal leader, Midir, as the Dalriads try to throw off the ritual of slavery imposed by Liadhan, the witch queen. Phaedrus accepts the challenge for it will bring meaning back into his life, or, as it says in the imagery of the book, it will give a new edge to the bluntness of his existence. Little does he know that it will bring him an all too brief period of comradeship and fulfilment as the "Horse Lord". Even more miraculously it will bring him the love of a woman who is the daughter of his enemy.

Most of the action takes place in what would be in present-day Argyll but the story begins in Corbridge and the sad but glorious climax comes back to the world where Roman power seems absolute. Captured by one of the Roman commanders, Phaedrus can only buy his freedom and the return to his pregnant wife and his now adoring people, by agreeing to hand over one thousand of his best young warriors to serve in the imperial army. Phaedrus shows he really has come home to his people, that he has in truth become the horse lord he pretended to be for so long, by the dreadful sacrifice he is prepared to make.

The Eagle of the Ninth is perhaps Rosemary Sutcliff's most famous book and the one that offers the most deeply satisfying story about Roman Britain. If offers the solution to an age-old mystery, it has the account of a quest which changes into a headlong chase, it details the development of a friendship that grows across the boundaries of Celt and Roman and it finally turns into a love story between two young people and the country that both have come to love. And, at the core of what is clearly Rosemary Sutcliff's masterpiece, there are two symbols that remain in the memory: one is the eagle that represents the transitory nature of power, honour and reputation; the other is the Roman Wall that conjures up the division of peoples, the road to danger on one side and the hope of safety on the other.

There are many legends that concern the Ninth Hispana legion which set out from York, marched north from Hadrian's Wall and never came back. Marcus, the hero of Sutcliff's story, is the son of the first cohort leader of the missing legion. He has to live with the stories of the possible cowardice and desertion that now accompany the name of the Ninth Hispana. His own courage is put to the test when as centurion and fort commander he saves his men from being overwhelmed in a rebellion at Isca Dumnoniorum (present-day Exeter). The wound he receives costs him his place in the Roman army and he becomes one of the typical Sutcliff heroes, a man without a place in the world that surrounds him. As he recovers at his uncle's house a whole series of inexplicable factors begin to work upon him to recall him to a life of purpose and fulfilment. First there is his friendship with Esca, a native Briton, whom he rescues after his defeat in the gladiatorial bout in the arena. Secondly, there is the affection he feels for the rescued wolf-cub which he rears as a family pet. Thirdly there is his ripening relationship with young Cottia, a girl from the Iceni tribe, who refuses to become the civilised and eligible Roman maiden that her aunt intends her to be.

For a while, however, more important than all of these attractions, is the chance to find out the truth about the Ninth Hispana and redeem the lost honour of his family. If he recovers the lost eagle it could prevent its being used as a rallying talisman for the tribes who might want to attack Hadrian's Wall, and it might even be possible to reform the legion and thus to put right what had gone wrong. Together Marcus and Esca set off for the Wall and the land to the north. Again we get a brief picture of life at the edifice that straddles the countryside and we trace for a while the journeys of the two men as they wander the countryside in search of clues. Even though he was raised in Clusium in Italy and has had little love for Britain, Marcus gradually begins to discover something about the land and the people which puts roots deep into his heart. He and Esca travel together not as master and slave but as friends and comrades. The people they must take the eagle back from may be enemies but they still have traditions and loyalties that must be appreciated. The survivor of the lost legion whom they find has assimilated himself into the ways of another country. The songs and ideas of his army days may stay with him but he has a wife and children in this new world.

Marcus and Esca flee from the chasing tribes and reach the safety of the wall near Housesteads. In terms of finding the eagle and bringing it back home the mission has been a success but Marcus has to abandon all hope about the Ninth Hispana coming back to life again. A part of what caused their defeat north of Hadrian's Wall was shameful and the whole story is bound to be covered up by the authorities in Rome. His own future is just as uncertain for he still has no occupation. A letter from the Senate transforms his fortunes – it gives him a pension and a land grant and the opportunity to return home to Italy. Suddenly Marcus knows what he wants – for, in some mysterious way, home has become Britain. He realises that home means the company of his uncle Aquila, the friendship of Esca and the love that he can now share with Cottia who will soon become his bride. He chooses land on the slopes of the South Downs but it is partly his experiences to the north of the wall that have drained the restlessness from his soul and given him a deeper understanding of his own and other people's feelings.

The Roman Wall – Civil War

As we trace further Winifred Cawley's **Feast of the Serpent** (22C – see page 21 for 22A and page 26 for 22B) we note that the story begins with a journey to find the Faa or gypsy people for the spring festival of the serpent. Adonell Heron's mother travels again to the places on the Roman Wall where she had first got to know her late husband. There, amidst the ruins of Roman forts and medieval castles, local moss-trooper warlords carry on the tradition of attacking travellers and dodging the soldiers sent out to find them. Of late, however, the punitive raids by the Parliamentary soldiers have become more efficient and brutal. The days of the border reivers are coming to an end.

As she is initiated into the rites of the Faa people by the waters of Crag Lough, Adonell realises that she is not being allowed to choose. Reluctantly she goes through with the

The loneliness of the wall near Crag Lough features in "Feast of the Serpent" by Winifred Cawley, "So Guy Came Too" by Lorna Hill, "Explorers on the Wall" by Garry Hogg and in "Wildcat Tower", the earliest of all Northumberland children's stories by G. Christopher Davies.

ceremony and is taught some of the skills of gypsy life. These include purse snatching, selling horses whose ages have been disguised and using deception and superstition to trick poor farm people out of their money and valuables. A chance encounter with Archie Rede at Alston starts to convince her that there are other things in life than a way of behaving that she finds despicable. When her mother dies there is nothing to tie her to her adopted gypsy family and she sets off to return home to Elsdon or to find Archie. But, as we saw in the Newcastle section, she succeeds in arriving in that town just in time for the infamous witch trials. Her ordeal has just begun.

The Roman Wall – Jacobites

The other, less successful, book by Elspeth Burn is ***Charles and the Fifteen*** – 1968 (82) a story about the 1715 Jacobite rebellion. It is set both down in the Tyne Valley between Hexham and Corbridge and in the uplands to the north, taking in such places as Capheaton and Barrasford. Journeys along old drove roads, the remains of Roman roads and on trails through the forested river valleys are described very well. Again a map at the front of the book allows you to follow the travels of Charles and Mary with some accuracy. This time, however, the reasons for crossing so much countryside in secrecy and in haste are not at all clear.

The trouble is that the political situation in 1715 is less capable of clear-cut explanation than life on a Roman frontier as shown in *Julian and the Wall.* There is no attempt at even-handedness as in the previous story and, during the narrative, the author appears to take it for granted that you will sympathise with what Charles and Mary are doing and that you will find Lord Derwentwater of Dilston Hall a sympathetic and tragic figure. The freedom Elspeth Burn gained by having totally fictional characters in *Julian and the Wall* has been lost in this tale about some real figures from history with whose motives and life-style not everybody will agree, nor indeed empathise at all, without a good deal more explanation. The author's note at the end strikes a more sober and realistic tone and the facts about what later happened to each of the personalities in her tale confirm indeed that it was a "sad little story".

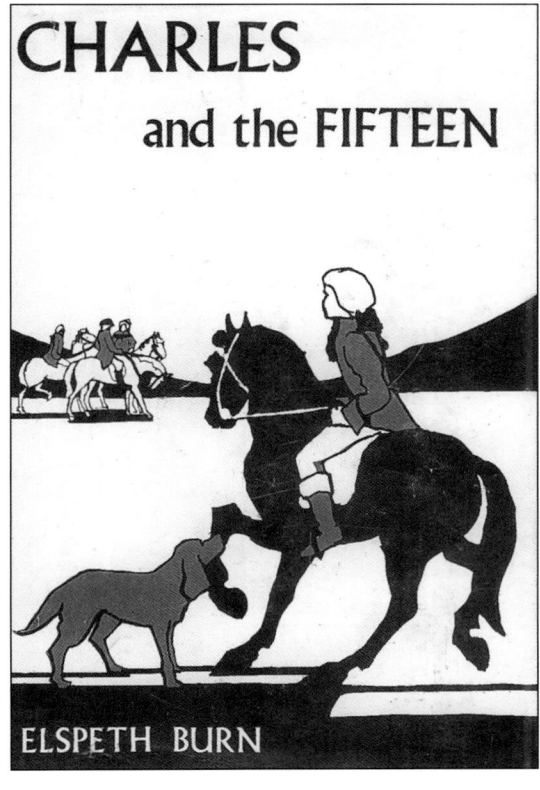

The Roman Wall – Modern Times

The Stolen Seasons – 1967 (83) by David Divine is a first-rate children's action story set both on and close to Hadrian's Wall. However, though the plot is very well crafted and the chase sequences full of tension, the author has also succeeded in taking his readers with him to a world of deeper feelings and larger ideas than those of mere transitory excitement. Amongst the author's other work is a detailed account of the military value of the Roman Wall and its effect on military campaigns. This solid background of historical knowledge and intimate acquaintance with the geography and geology of the small area around Housesteads means that every movement of every character in the book can be believed in with confidence. As you read the book you feel that he has walked every step of the way and seen the landscape from every angle by both day and night. More than anything else David Divine has thought about what this frontier country means now and what it has meant in the past. From these thoughts he has developed a book with two plots which are both divided and linked by the extraordinary wall itself.

The first question that he poses is "Did the wall work ?" Was it possible for a small group of determined tribesmen to scale the wall and infiltrate and raid the country beyond ? Without waiting to discuss the pros and cons of this idea the author plunges his three children into the thick of the action. They are the raiders who must try to penetrate the modern day wall from the north. A bet with a professor of archaeology conducting a "dig" just to the south of the wall is part of the challenge. If the "raiders" are seen at all by any inhabitant of the countryside then the wager is lost. There are other rules of fairness that the writer introduces as the story bowls along at top speed: rivers have to be forded, farmers' dogs have to be kept upwind, fire-watchers in tall towers have to be crept past using the folds in the countryside, the present crumbling wall has to be climbed in daylight when someone is actually walking along it and it all must be clambered over within a certain number of seconds.

Peter Manson and his sister Mig, with their American friend, Clinton, first start their journey fourteen miles away. To replace the local knowledge that the barbarian tribesmen would have had Peter has studied the local Ordnance Survey map until he feels it is written on the inside of his brain. It needs to be – for, to make the test valid, he cannot use it. The time taken to swing a grapnel and climb the rope attached over a wall the original height and thickness of Hadrian's has been calculated by practices on the roof of a boat shed. The point of assault between each milecastle has been worked out by the lie of the land and the time taken by patrolling sentries. Even the prongs of the grapnel had been covered in canvas to simulate the sheepskin that would have been used to deaden the sound of its landing on the masonry. The children are scrupulously honest and, even when Mig creeps into the ruined villa and stands next to Professor Carrick for a whole minute before he realises she is there, they are prepared to re-consider their success when they spot someone watching the "dig". Could he have seen them on their secret climb over the wall ?

At this point the wall has been crossed and the bet has seemingly been won. It is then that the book suddenly takes off in a new and unexpected direction. Within the small ruined villa there are signs of a fire, perhaps the result of a raid which confirms the theory that the wall could have been penetrated. Lodged in a collapsed wall is a metal dish and the team of archaeologists work meticulously to record its position and then remove the large stones that trap it in place. It is work that will take days. The children are allowed to watch and do minor tasks to help in the excavation. Alongside the dish is a gap that is too small for the grown-ups to put their hands through. Mig is invited to insert her fingers and to explore what is on the reverse side of the metal. In the best scene in the book David Divine brings out wonderfully how she connects with the metal and also with the past as, eyes closed, she reveals what she can feel to the spellbound team of professionals. Clearly a precious work of great beauty will be given to the world when the work of careful extraction is complete.

That night, however, professional thieves cosh the man on guard duty and crudely prise the dish out of the wall with the crowbar. Other antiquities have been stolen at other sites but this would be the greatest treasure of them all. Peter, Mig and Clint blunder across the crime and Mig manages to seize the dish and set off into the darkness. The whole of the first part of the book is now turned on its head. The three children are back over the wall and on the run. They are no longer playing a game; they are being pursued by callous and ruthless criminals. All they have to help them is their recently acquired detailed local knowledge and the hours of darkness. It gradually emerges that the men chasing them are ex-commandos and that they are led by the Captain, a man who has no intention of ever giving up. The pursuit that follows is chilling in its reality. The plight of the children is made more desperate when it is seen through the eyes of the father as he gradually realises just what is happening. The climax, which it would not be fair to reveal, takes place on an island in the middle of a peat bog.

As the book closes the reader becomes aware that there has been more than an exciting adventure contained in its pages. There has also been a rare insight into the nature of the countryside, the people who lived there in the past and the way in which both professional archaeologists and ordinary people can develop both a scientific and instinctive understanding of the former inhabitants of this partly-lost world. The "Seasons" of the title refers to the pictures that Mig found on the reverse of the Roman plate and the reader is convinced of the beauty of the artefact by the resilience that she shows in fighting to preserve it from being "stolen" for ever. As the author's one book for children set in this region, it too is worth preserving for future generations to read.

The most prolific writer from the north-east region is, of course, Catherine Cookson. Most of her stories are set in South Tyneside. However, a brief mention should be made of her children's book *Lanky Jones* – 1980 (84), for it starts when Lanky and his father become snowbound on a farm near Bardon Mill and the strange behaviour of each member of the Everton family diverts them for a while from their own troubles. The resolution of the story, as you might expect, takes place on the south bank of the Tyne near South Shields. *Matty Doolin* – 1965 (85), also by Cookson, is another tale that belongs by rights to the South Tyneside area but concerns what happens when three boys from the city are transplanted to a farm somewhere in the hills beyond Hexham.

It is a sad fact that sometimes explanations can lead to let-downs. Nowhere is it more true than in Winifred Finlay's books where the voyage into the puzzle is more intriguing and frightening and pleasurable than the eventual quick release from the bonds of the plot and the escape from the well-developed oppressive atmosphere. *Danger at Black Dyke* – 1968 (86) is a perfect example of this phenomenon. This is set in wild, marshy countryside surrounding the Roman Wall between Chollerford and Housesteads. Three young boys, Geordie, Hamish and Tim have formed their own First Cohort of the Tungrian legion and, taking their inspiration from the nearby temple at Carrawburgh, they have declared themselves Men of Mithras. They have even taken the Lion and Raven masks, created in their art classes at school, and regularly patrol the wall looking for trouble and adventure. Thus when Bud, a young American student stumbles (literally) into their territory, they are on hand to deal with him in an appropriate manner. For all his dour and harsh exterior it is eleven year old Geordie who has the greatest compassion for the stranger. Bud's plight triggers something in his own memory that brings back the despair on the lonely streets of Newcastle. Geordie's own history is gradually teased out into the story-line whilst the forces that menace the mysterious Bud gradually close in on the old cottage at Black Dyke.

Tourists at Chesters and youth hostellers at Once Brewed lead to a description of Geordie's thoughts and feelings as he waits to make contact with the friends whom Bud wants to thank. As he cycles determinedly along the Military Road Geordie's mind swings between the past and the present; from the moss-troopers and the Romans to the young man called Craig and and his sister Debbie and the sinister followers whom he dubs "The Yellow Peril" and "Smiler". The mystery of why Bud is on the run seems only to be getting deeper. Meanwhile Bud, hobbling about on his own, has an encounter with Geordie's grandmother who takes him for a wealthy tourist staying at the George in Chollerford. In a rich and colourful northern dialect she warns him about getting off the track and about the haunting of Black Dyke itself.

In the end the villains are, of course, sent packing by the redoubtable old lady and a fearsome white bull called King Arthur. By this time, however, we are much more interested in the story of Geordie, the details of which have slowly been revealed. His mother died and his father didn't want him and left for Canada. Only his grandmother was prepared to take him in and she had watched his recovery from this abandonment with some concern. The way in which he befriended Tim and Hamish and formed his secret Men of Mithras showed the resilience of his character. However, the fragility of his imaginary world gradually disintegrates under the pressure of the very real danger from the mysterious strangers. When Tim and Hamish want Debbie to join their special legion he feels as if his carefully built new life has been ruthlessly smashed. It is Debbie herself who is able to reach out to him by describing how she has lost her brother to the world of adults and how she understands how things can never be the same. Geordie, for the first time, is able to tell someone of what it feels like not to be wanted. Debbie convinces him that, though Tim and Hamish have defied him, they still admire and respect him. For the first time Geordie realises that there is something about girls that he can like and appreciate and, when he returns from his tear-stained isolation, he is a boy renewed in spirit and the strongest advocate of Debbie joining his very special gang.

The reasons that Bud is on the run are finally explained but the reader understands very quickly that the story of South American revolution has merely been a literary device to set this Roman Wall story in motion and to explore the character of Geordie.

Three 'D's on Hadrian's Wall – 1959 (87) by Gordon Grinstead is one of those strange hybrid books that get produced when an educational publisher spots an opportunity to mix instruction with entertainment. In this case it is one volume in the Cassell's Silver Circle Reader series, and a study of the end-papers makes it clear that the "Three 'D's" in question have other adventures in other parts of the country. Indeed some of these are referred to during the course of this text.

Basically, the sort of information that you would find in a guidebook about the most well-known features of the Roman Wall is woven into a tale of a wages snatch in Newcastle and the concealment of the loot on an identified archaeological site. In fact there are four characters whose names begin with "D" in this story. Dick and Diana are the adventurous

WINIFRED CAWLEY

Down the Long Stairs

Winifred Cawley's earlier novel of the Second Civil War is set in 1648 and is the exciting story of fifteen-year-old Ralph Cole, the son of a wealthy coal merchant who died fighting for the king. In a rash moment Ralph's anger and bitterness at his mother's intended marriage to a Parliament man leads him to leave his comfortable home and join the Royalist garrison at Tynemouth Castle. But there is little time for regrets, for with the storming of the castle and his own miraculous escape, Ralph's life becomes that of a fugitive pursued through Northumberland by the Roundheads—and in particular by his old enemy Harbottle Grimston—with the knowledge that his capture could mean slavery in Barbados or Venice.

'The book gives an excellent portrait of everyday life and conditions among north-country workers in the small pits and cottages of Northumberland. The author deserves special commendation for the way she has shown the emotions and attitudes of a fifteen-year-old under stress and when confronted by different loyalties.'

The School Librarian

ILLUSTRATED BY WILLIAM STOBBS

Jacket illustration by Doreen Roberts for "Feast of the Serpent" (OUP 1969) by Winifred Cawley, reprinted by permission of Oxford University Press.

The Temple of Mithras, which inspired Geordie and his followers in "Danger at Black Dyke".

The famous "George Inn" at Chollerford which features in both "Danger at Black Dyke" and several Lorna Hill stories where she sometimes renamed it as "The Dragon".

and inquisitive children at the heart of the action. Their dog, who often lives up to his name by carrying out unofficial excavations, is called Digger. The children's Uncle Don, a young archaeologist, provides the adult supervision as they visit various different parts of the country.

From very early on it is clear what the assigned roles are in terms of the way in which the author seeks to impart information and understanding to the pupils who read his book. Uncle Don is very much the teacher and Dick and Diana are his "victims". It is not that they are not both intelligent and curious; it's just that they have to sit through some rather lengthy and dry explanations. He sometimes even tells them, when they are bursting with vital information about someone interfering with his "dig", that they should wait until he has finished and not interrupt. More amusingly, when the end of the book goes into "chase" mode, and they are being driven at top speed through the Northumberland countryside on the way to Holy Island, Uncle Don still persists in dropping more snippets of historical information, as they thunder round bends and watch the circling helicopter close in on the thieves. Clearly, no matter how heart-stopping the situation, no opportunity for education must be neglected.

The facts about Housesteads and the temple of Mithras at Carrawburgh are presented clearly and concisely. The exact purpose of items in the old places of worship are discussed in an inviting and graphic fashion. The old professor even lies down in one of the ancient tomb-like stone boxes to try to prove his theory. On one occasion the children blunder across a wild-looking tattooed man, collapsed in a new temple that is due to be excavated, and it seems as if the past has suddenly come alive in an inexplicable and frightening way.

However, very strangely, having achieved a certain amount of dramatic grip, the author appears to have decided to play safe by allowing the inclusion of other features that remind his readers that it is all "just a story". The very sketchy and rather implausible outline of the Newcastle robbery plot is the first of these. More striking, however, is the choice of the names assigned to the different characters. Thus the rival archaeologist is identified as Professor Moonhead, the woman at whose cottage they stay is called Mrs. Cowcake, the helicopter pilot is Captain Flyte and the criminal mastermind behind the vicious attack and robbery is constantly referred to as Mr. Big. The criminal gang say "Mr.Big" and the author writes, without a glimmer of irony, sentences about how "Big" makes his various moves. The dialogue, particularly that between the "goodies" and "baddies" contains a string of stock expressions that contrast badly with the well targeted vocabulary of the educational descriptions. It certainly jars when we learn that "The game's up" and that "the old buffer", otherwise Professor Moonhead, is safe.

Nevertheless, in spite of some rather stilted sections, the book still achieves its primary purpose and would leave any young reader better informed about so many things connected with the Romans in the north-east. Any deficiencies in the other parts of the story-line can reasonably be assigned to having to cram so much into the formula and length required by the series editor.

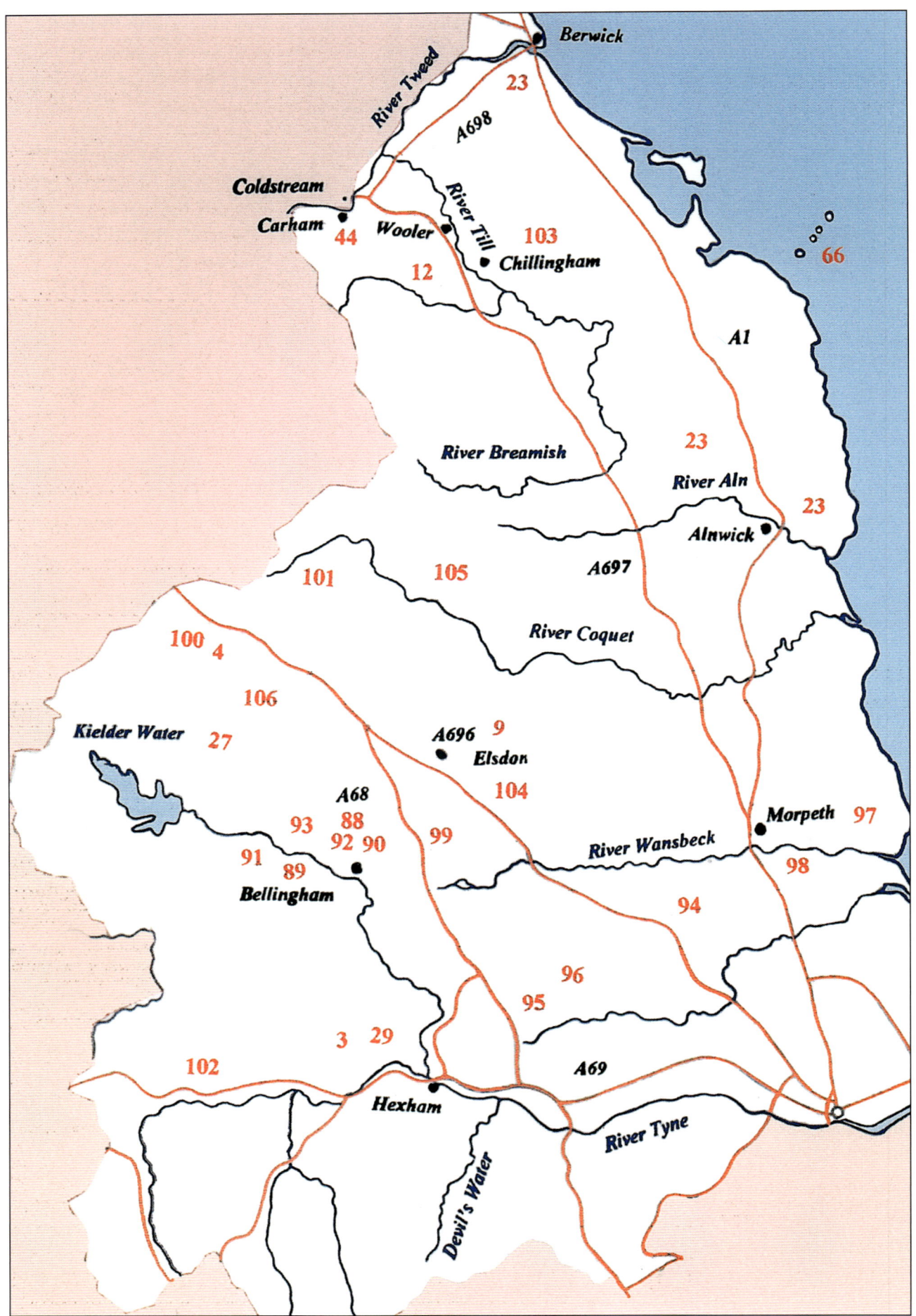

Berwick

River Tweed

A698 23

Coldstream

Carham 44 Wooler

River Till

103

Chillingham

12

66

A1

River Breamish

23

River Aln

23

Alnwick

101 105

A697

River Coquet

100 4

106

Kielder Water 27

A696 9

Elsdon

A68

104

93 88

92 90

99

Morpeth 97

91

89

River Wansbeck

98

Bellingham

94

96

95

3 29

102

A69

Hexham

River Tyne

Devil's Water

76

Stage 4: In Deepest Northumberland

THE books listed below can be found on the map but in many cases their precise location is no more than conjecture. Some writers simply wanted a Northumberland story and took care to disguise actual names by their own inventions. It is also worth pointing out that these books are sometimes merely the representatives of a writer's work. Thus all the titles by Kim Lewis and Lorna Hill would overcrowd particular stretches of the countryside near Bellingham. Not every detail of Winifred Finlay's or L.E.O. Charlton's stories of the Middle Marches, nor the journeys made by Julian Atterton's wandering harpers and knights can be fixed by a neat piece of numbering. Similarly it would be pleasant to write more about Marjorie and Esmé in their mannequin parade at a shop in Morpeth (and Guy's reaction to it !) but Lorna Hill has already occupied her fair share of these pages. So, to ensure as complete an account as possible, the other "Northumberland" stories that have scenes in this region are listed at the foot of this page.

97. The Whinstone Drift –
Richard Armstrong

88. Just Like Floss – Kim Lewis
89. Emma's Lamb – Kim Lewis
90. My Friend Harry – Kim Lewis
91. First Snow – Kim Lewis
92. One Summer Day – Kim Lewis
93. The Last Train – Kim Lewis
94. Jenny's Adventure – Ursula Ridley
95. The Secret of the Border Castle – Angela Brazil
96. The Nameless Pony – Catherine Carey
97. The Whinstone Drift – Richard Armstrong
98. Gallowa – Mike Kirkup
99. The Secret of the Peel – L.E.O. Charlton
100. The Camp at Auld Man Shiel – L.E.O. Charlton
4B. The Hut on Oh Me Edge – L.E.O. Charlton
66. The Mystery of Cowsole Wood – L.E.O. Charlton
101. Martin Farrell – Janni Howker
102. The House with No Windows – Allan Jermieson
9. The Witch of Redesdale – Winifred Finlay
27. Mystery in the Middle Marches – Winifred Finlay
12. Storm Over Cheviot – Winifred Finlay
103. The Courage of Andy Robson – Frederick Grice
104. The Secret of Rumbling Churn – John Sweet
29. Dress Rehearsal – Lorna Hill
3. Jane Leaves the Wells – Lorna Hill
105. Veronica at the Wells – Lorna Hill
106. Dancing Peel – Lorna Hill
44. Knights of the Sacred Blade – Julian Atterton
23. Ransom for a Knight – Barbara Leonie Picard

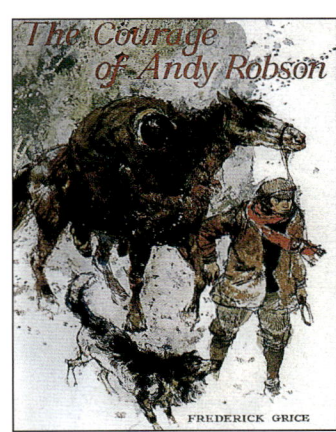

Jacket illustration (1969)
by Victor Ambrus, reprinted
by permission of OUP.

The Other Stories

Secret Heart – David Almond

Border Peel, So Guy Came Too, They Called her Patience, Masquerade at the Wells, No Castanets at the Wells, Ella at the Wells, Return to the Wells, Back Stage, Dancer's Luck – Lorna Hill.

Floss, The Shepherd Boy, Days on the Farm, A Quilt for Baby, Little Lamb, Friends, Little Calf, Little Puppy, Little Baa – Kim Lewis.

Curse on the Sea – Geoffrey Trease (Characters pass through on the way to Scotland and back)

Somewhere in Northumberland – the Picture Books

SOMEWHERE near Bellingham in Northumberland is the working sheep farm where Kim Lewis writes and illustrates the books for very young children that have been shared by countless parents and boys and girls around the world. She draws what she sees around her and provides us with an intimate portrait of farm life in the remote rural north-east. Her principal character is Floss, the sheepdog who has a major role to play in some of the books and who makes small guest appearances in others. The natural rhythms of the countryside: the routine of each day, the passing of the seasons, the birth of young animals and their growth to maturity, are all part of the cycle of stories that reflect different stages in the development of very young children.

In *Just Like Floss* (88) our familiar friend is old enough to have puppies and, of course the children on the farm want to know if they may keep them. A gentle reality is then introduced into the story when the father declares that only one is needed to work with Floss and to look after the sheep. When the smallest puppy, Sam, strays into the field one day he refuses to be cowed by the sheep who gather threateningly round him. It is the magic moment when his destiny is decided. His spark of courage is enough to make him the chosen work companion of Floss, his mother, in the future. *Emma's Lamb* – 1991 (89) tells the story of a lost lamb who is brought home for the little girl of the house to look after. Emma has a lot of fun feeding the lamb and then playing games with it. However, the story ends with Emma happily accepting that she can't look after the lamb for ever and that it must return to its mother.

In *My Friend Harry* –1995 (90) Kim Lewis unites two ideas that are very important in the lives of young children. First there is the friendship and love that a child may invest in a favourite toy companion. Secondly there is the way in which the child begins to realise that life is a series of little bridges to cross as their world expands to places outside the home. On the second day of nursery school James is ready to take his stuffed elephant with him so that they both draw upon the help and the warmth of their long companionship.

Always there are the evocative drawings of the countryside. *First Snow* – 1993 (91) takes Sara, her mother and her teddy up into the hills where they can look past the bent lone pine tree and across the drystone wall to what must be the greys and yellows of the distant Cheviots. Then, suddenly, across the valley in the next picture you can see the sky turn white. Sara and her mother struggle to spread the straw for the hillside sheep before the storm catches them. On the way back a minor tragedy looms. Teddy has been left behind and there is picture of Sara sitting defiantly and miserably still in the snow. The day is saved by the arrival of one of the sheepdogs carrying the teddy safely in his mouth. Then it's home to the warm fire and the arms of her Daddy. The last picture shows us the same scene past the old pine tree and the drystone wall; the distant hills are now cream and white and blue with the snow and ice. *One Summer Day* – 1996 (92) where toddler Max goes for a walk with his grown-up friend Sara, shows some of the same countryside in summer. There is the lushness of the grass, the shadows of the tree-lined lane and blue sky reflected in the swiftly running river.

In *The Last Train* – 1994 (93) young Sara and James discover yet another new dimension to the familiar countryside that lies around them. The trains that used to run by the farm are long gone but the old stone railroad cottage is still there as a reminder. Kim Lewis makes the past meet the present and chronicles the growth of a child's imagination as from out of the distance the children visualise the old steam train roaring down the track once again.

Kim Lewis says that she now has to use photographs to recapture what her own children were once like so that she can use them in her stories. It is a mark of the passing of time. However, her stories and her pictures are one of the best attempts you are ever likely to find at capturing both the magical kingdoms of early childhood and some special places in the Northumberland countryside that are still out there to be rediscovered.

Somewhere in Northumberland – The Peel Tower

Jenny's Adventure – 1967 (94) by Ursula Ridley is one of those books that appears to be rambling along through a series of episodic happenings and then suddenly, in the last few chapters, develops an organised plot and even addresses quite a serious theme. This approach to fiction is not necessarily an ineffective one for the reader gets to know both the central characters, and those that surround them very well indeed before increasing the drama and the tension. On some occasions the very ordinariness of what has gone before makes events towards the end of the story more plausible as they emerge from what has become everyday reality for the reader.

Jenny Dacre belongs to a relatively well-off upper middle class family who live in a Peel Tower in Northumberland. This affluence is established by the fact that she and her younger siblings have a nanny and by the information that her brother travels away to public school. It is a protected world where, even at an early age, culture and learning are given a high value by the family. There are also the opportunities for exciting adventures that draw upon all the traditions and legends of the north-east of England. Thus the children delight in playing the games of border raiders, using sticks to represent cattle that can be stolen. The adults conspire in promoting this fun by having cows carved out of wood but the boys prefer to use them as targets for their bows and arrows.

Most of the well-known stories (and some of the hardly known) of Northumberland emerge as Jenny describes her life and the people her family know. However, because they are told with the frankness and naïvety of an eleven year old, they acquire a new charm and allure. A perfect example of this is the tradition of climbing on to a chair and jumping into the New Year. Jenny notices that some of the ladies climb up but apparently get frightened of jumping down. She has already begun to notice that they rather enjoy being helped back to safety by young men ! Similarly she recounts the stories of the Delavals of Delaval Hall and enigmatically mentions the story of how one lord died because he was "fatally kicked by a laundry maid". It seems an odd snippet of information for a young girl to treasure in her mind. On the other hand when Jenny and her family visit Housesteads with Professor Hammond she makes it clear that they were all pretty bored with the unimpressive set of ruins that remain. Even the so-called "Murder Room" holds no fascination for her. Then, suddenly, and amusingly for the reader, all the prudishness of childhood is summed up by her repugnance towards the idea of all the Roman legionaries sitting together on the row of holes of the communal loo.

There are other aspects of childhood that are convincingly and economically conveyed. For Jenny a visit to a deep mine becomes like a journey into hell and the mundane idea of descending in a lift and leaving your tummy behind works well in the mouth of a young girl. The remorseless logic of childhood makes her wonder about grown-ups who, not having seen her for a while, always comment on the fact that she has grown. As she points out it really would be something more remarkable to comment on if she hadn't grown. Another habitual saying about family resemblance:

"Your mother will never be dead while you're alive…"

also has to be examined in all its layers before she realises exactly what is meant.

Eventually the book begins to unfold the plot and the adventure that Jenny has been hinting at from the very first page. Archaeology may have its dull moments at Hadrian's

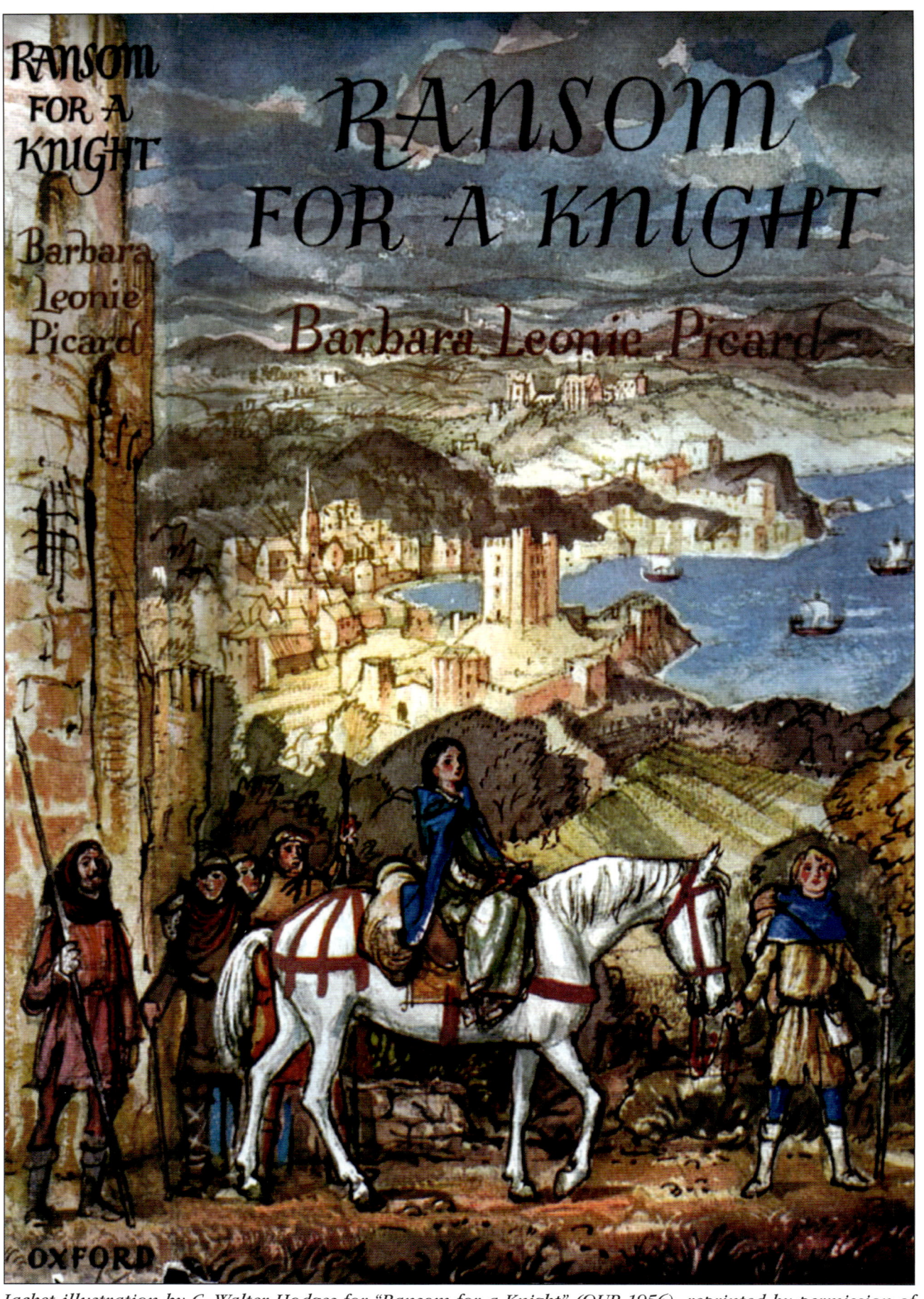

Jacket illustration by C. Walter Hodges for "Ransom for a Knight" (OUP 1956), reprinted by permission of Oxford University Press.

Wall but there is something very attractive about an excavation on the land near to your home. Jenny's father suggests the investigation of a depression he has noticed in a field nearby and, when the labour of digging proves too arduous for the combined efforts of his family and their friends, he actually gets a former pitman and his marra to do the hard work. Here the author cannot resist interposing a short section on colliery myths and stories which yields the interesting information that some miners actually used to suck on a piece of coal because they believed it helped if you had breathing problems. However, Ursula Ridley quickly returns to the main plot. What the two pitmen uncover is in fact the remains of an old drift mine which is eventually turned into a playroom for the children.

It is in this drift mine that Jenny finds Jim Wilson one day. He is a boy on the run from an approved school and, threatened by violence, Jenny agrees not to give him away. Secretly she rather likes the idea of building him into her fantasies about border ballads and Scottish prisoners. She is happy to supply him with food and water. She lets her cousin, Arabella, in on the idea and the two of them even get together to put on a village concert to raise money so that Jim can get to London and see his mother. When Arabella betrays the truth to her parents the full weight of the law descends on both him and the luckless girls who have tried to help him.

The story ends with a court case in Newcastle in which Jenny and Arabella have to face up to the consequences of what they have done by harbouring someone who is wanted by the law. Ignorance and youth can be no defence unless they have learned their lesson. There is a strong sense of the family bonding together round them whilst at the same time trying to help out Jim. Both the girls and the young man are meant to realise that you can't run away from your problems. It is better to face up to them and not live in a world of hopes and pretence.

The first-person narrator may only be eleven but the writer has effectively conveyed one of those experiences that she is likely to remember for the rest of her life. The fact that it all grew out of an orderly and loving and privileged world that has been plausibly and carefully established makes it seem even more real.

Somewhere in Northumberland – the School Story

She pronounced her name to rhyme with "dazzle" whilst previous generations of her family were quite content to sound like the country. Without doubt Angela Brazil is one of the "big four" writers who have become synonymous with the genre of school stories for girls. Her output was unusual in that, unlike the other three writers bracketed with her in terms of popularity and notoriety: Elsie J. Oxenham, Dorita Fairlie Bruce and Elinor M. Brent Dyer, she rarely used the same girls or the same schools twice. This is true again of ***The Secret of the Border Castle*** – 1943 (95) where Vanessa Wilson, her thirteen and a half year old heroine, makes her one and only appearance. So far as can be traced this is also the sole time that Angela Brazil wrote about Northumberland.

The catalyst for the visit to this remote part of England was the Second World War and the need for large numbers of children to be evacuated from the areas suffering from the Blitz. Vanessa Wilson, whose mother is dead and whose father is in the R.A.F. but later posted "missing", is determined to stay with her younger brother whose nerves have been shattered by the German bombing. Young Donald is to be sent away to a small preparatory school in the quiet of rural Northumberland and Vanessa is determined to follow. She persuades Miss Selkirk, her temporary guardian, to allow her to join "The Pines", one of the local girls' schools that is relocating to the gate-house of Langdon Castle in Northumberland. In order to make ends meet Miss Holt, the headmistress and owner of the Pines, is taking in boarders from other local schools where the parents are anxious for their girls to be safely out of the way.

From this opening situation Angela Brazil then begins to weave together three or four of the usual strands of the stock material of girls' school stories. Firstly there is the "rival schools having to come together" thread where old loyalties, old traditions and old friendships all have to be put into the melting pot of a new situation. Secondly, there is the story of the "outsider" where Vanessa, normally "a good mixer", belongs to neither faction. Thirdly – and this sort of story could hardly do without it – there is a mystery belonging to Langdon Castle and it in some way involves a missing will and Vanessa's own family. Finally, there is the story of loss and re-discovery concerning Vanessa, young Donald and her beloved father.

The location itself is that interesting mixture of the fictional and the real with the towns and villages sometimes identified and sometimes uncannily reminiscent of the real wartime Britain where the signposts have been dug out and removed in case a German spy could find his way around too easily. Thus it is difficult to make much of the descriptions of Bewburn and Kirklands Cross which both seem to be on the border with Scotland and yet still very close to the Roman Wall. However, journeys to Hexham and the different Roman forts on the Wall itself are given plausible walking timetables and identifiable landscape features. Vanessa herself proves a girl sensitive to the history of her surroundings and daydreams about the moss-troopers of the old raiding days.

However, in spite of the contributions of all the above material to the content of the book, the texture, colour and depth of the final picture are provided by something that was very dear to the author's heart in this and many other of her books. It is a form of practical morality, of doing good, that Angela Brazil must surely have seen as her essential contribution to the national spirit. To clarify what is being suggested it is worthwhile taking a close look at Mrs. Roper, the wife of the local doctor, and the effect that she has on "The Gate-house Girls".

"Here, in the midst of this great war they're occupied with their own silly little quarrels, instead of uniting to think of how to serve their country. Can't I persuade them to rise to a higher level ?"

Mrs. Roper has enough subtlety and wisdom to realise that a group of girls suddenly cast into the middle of the remote countryside far from any of their usual entertainment, rationed even to the number of books that they can read, will need far more than mere education if they are to grow as human beings and become "future citizens of the empire". After getting the girls to appreciate each others' qualities by the way which she puts them into tennis teams, she embarks upon her grander plan of building them into a useful organisation that could make a contribution to the war effort whilst allowing them to have fun at the same time. In essence, of course, she is talking about the formation of a group like the Girl Guides or the Camp Fire Girls. Strangely enough the author herself never belonged to such an organisation but stories involving both the principles and the practical activities of "guiding" groups were a part of the staple diet of girls' school stories in the 1920s and 1930s.

In this book the theme of "doing your duty" is saved from becoming overpoweringly and off-puttingly pious by the fact that it is set during wartime. The girls in the book have sisters who are Wrens, WAAFs and Land Girls, and some of them have brothers and fathers who are fighting a war to the death with Hitler. There is some point in learning to do First Aid and learning to read the lie of the countryside when it could very well be your turn next.

Thus the whole of the middle section of the book concerns Mrs. Roper's efforts to both educate and entertain the intermediate girls of the school. Angela Brazil at this point manages to cram in lots of interesting information about the Roman Wall and she even has Mrs. Roper tell a story within a story, recapturing what life must have been like for an upper-class lady living on the frontier of civilisation. Later visits take them to Hexham and Corbridge and the history of the two towns is told to the reader as Mrs. Roper tells it to the girls. The girls compare in their own minds the retreat of the harassed English into their peel towers with the 1940s citizens of London sheltering from the Luftwaffe's bombs. However, in spite of these valiant attempts at contemporary relevance, when Angela Brazil begins on the detailed story of how Christianity came to Northumbria, and then produces her own versions of Border legends and ballads, you realise that she has certainly been assiduous in her research but has somehow neglected the need for more pace in the plot.

As the end of the book approaches and the well-worn clichés of the returned father and the discovery of the will make their clumsy presence felt, the author is less at ease with events in the world of wartime. The consolation offered to Vanessa when her father is on the missing list seems incredibly fanciful and inappropriate to the modern reader, and the girl's steady stoicism in the face of tragedy is remarkably implausible.

The Secret of Border Castle contains a wealth of information about Northumberland scenes and Northumbrian stories, and certain situations certainly possess both tension and charm. It is not untypical of Angela Brazil's prolific writing for girls, which, in its heydey, proved extremely popular. However, nowadays, though boarding school stories with updated settings can still capture a devoted audience, as Anne Digby's "Trebizon" stories have proved, the long digressions, the obsession with duty and the almost fairy-tale attitude to Christianity, all clearly belong to a "lost domain" that even adults would only revisit out of intellectual curiosity.

The Pony Story
The Nameless Pony by Catherine Carey (96) was published in 1972 by the Lutterworth Press in the "Crown Pony Series". An examination of the titles printed on the dustwrapper – *Only One Pony, Show-Jumping Summer, Because of a Pony* and *Clear Round for Katy* – shows us immediately that pony stories are a routine part of publishing life and they are, in spite of a decline in recent years, still popular with a large number of young girls. It would not be unfair to say that *The Nameless Pony* is a good representative of this genre of literature which just happens to be set in Northumberland.

Shelley, the first-person narrator of the story, is a book-worm who is totally lacking a sense of humour. She is horrified to find that she is to spend the summer at Bellnan in Northumberland with cousins whom she has never met. True, she is to live in an old peel tower with interesting historical associations, but, to her horror, she finds she is expected to learn how to ride and to cope with life in the country. This includes standing up to two enormous wolf-hounds that playfully knock her down every time they see her.

By the end of the book she is a child transformed. She has fallen in love with the Northumberland countryside, formed a happy relationship with a nice pony and made friends with her two cousins. She has also found the Shelton Treasure in a secret room which has eluded people's searches for over one hundred years ! Details of pony training are actually quite restricted. There are brief accounts of the usual fears and blunders associated with riding and sketchy details of outings in the Northumberland fields and moors. Shelley's success depends not so much on acquiring technique but on developing the right attitude. A medical crisis for her uncle, involving a dash to Newcastle, cements Shelley's place within the family circle and allows her to blossom as a good friend to her cousin in her time of need. This is a warm friendly book, where there are no villains and where even the sadness suggested by the nameless pony of the title is actually pleasantly misleading. Shelley's time of trial appears brief but her discovery of the joys of laughter is actually given greater prominence than the reversal of the Shelton fortunes by the finding of the long-lost treasure.

The Mining Story

The Whinstone Drift – 1951 (97) by Richard Armstrong deals with the mining industry in a Northumbrian valley. Once again, like the factory in *Sabotage at the Forge* (which could be his namesake's Lord Armstrong's factory), the actual valley is not precisely tied to a particular place in Northumberland or Durham. There are lots of clues about the actual location of the Whindyke Pit and the small village of Dewley: we learn it is in a small valley close to the sea, cut across by a huge limestone ridge, a small farm and a river. Two roads and a railway which runs through deep tunnels and cuttings are the only ways in and out. It is a place where nature meets industry with the traces of the village green and the old pantiled roofs of the farm labourers jostling alongside the spoil heap of the pit and the rows of miners' cottages. Relics of the past dominate the present and, for a while, look like they hold the key to the future. There is the blackened ruin of an old coal-owner's mansion; there is even a typical folly – a one hundred and fifty foot column with the figure of a man on the top and, somewhere in the valley, the remains of the Dorothy May Pit, the scene of the valley's greatest disaster.

Back to the valley after three years at school in the south of England comes sixteen year old Peter Musgrave, a boy who very soon has to make a decision about his future. The choice is between staying in Dewley and accepting the life of the pit or of working to gain a place in university. The reader soon realises that both pathways are fraught with difficulties that define themselves more clearly as each day passes and Peter tries to fit himself back into the life of the valley. The first problem is the more easily understood, for Peter and his two teenage friends soon find out that the rumour about the closure of the pit is true. The deposits of coal are nearly worked out and the great Whindyke lies in the way of exploiting new reserves on the farther side towards the sea. Peter's second route to a new life is blocked even more firmly by his total lack of enthusiasm for academic work and the absence of any real reason for going to university. He doesn't even know which course he would choose.

Throughout the book Peter wrestles with the difficulties of making the right decision and the author cleverly links the exploration of the valley and the forbidden manor house with the voyage that the young man makes inside himself. Several interesting themes are developed, a particularly compelling one being about the nature of friendship. The memory of early schooldays shared allows Peter to resume some sort of relationship with Jacko Harrison and Jim "Lanky" Linthouse. After a few false starts he even gets a chance to prove himself anew to the small community by his skill and commitment in an important football match. Eventually it dawns on Peter that what is keeping them apart is that, in spite of their ages being the same, the other two boys are given meaning and purpose in their lives both by the jobs they have taken up and the studies they pursue. A trip to the bottom of Whindyke Pit and conversations with sympathetic mine deputies and supervisors begins to show that intelligence and learning are just as much needed as practical skills and brute strength. There is a future for a young man who wants to dedicate himself to the work and the study.

Towards the end of the book, having got his readers thoroughly hooked by the story, Richard Armstrong begins to demonstrate that special quality in his writing that marks him out as a very talented writer. It is perhaps best described as the ability to make explanations of life and work in complicated industrial environments both clear and interesting. The various jobs in the metal-working industry came alive in *Sabotage at the Forge* and in *The Whinstone Drift* the variety and multiplicity of activities in the mine are laid out in such a way that we are convinced by each telling detail. In both cases Armstrong is trying to capture the feeling that each person is doing a job that is worthwhile, that there is a strange and compelling satisfaction of belonging to something that is bigger than yourself. Comradeship and purpose are a part of it all and that was why pit communities were so strong. Peter knows that he must prove himself worthy of inclusion in this world and so, with a new determination and pride, he sets out to solve the secret that can save the valley.

It would be fair to say that the resolution of the mystery and the clearing-up of what motivated the person the boys are contending with are more routine schoolboy mystery materials than something which springs naturally from real life. However, in spite of his warm picture of the people in the pit community, Armstrong gives us sympathetic glimpses of the countryside that was there before the coal was dug and we can understand the reluctance of one powerful individual to yield yet more territory to King Coal.

Ashington

Gallowa: the story of a pit pony – 1992 (98) by Mike Kirkup takes us once more to the Northumberland coalfield. This time the year is 1947 and the Labour government have nationalised the mining industry. But the same harsh conditions, the same comradeship and the same dangers still apply to Jimmy Stott starting on his career at the age of fifteen down the pit in Ashington. The really smart boys in Ashington get a job at the Co-op or one of the other stores in the small town but Jimmy is determined to follow in the footsteps of his father who has been pensioned off with the well-known "miners' disease" or pneumoconiosis. The story is on a small scale, just 72 pages and some of them are whole page illustrations.

"Gallowa" is not the name of one pony; it is the Galloway breed that is being referred to in the title. There are 42 ponies in the stables down the pit and the one about whose fate we become concerned is called Frank. In fact each of the ponies is usually given a one-syllable name that can be barked out followed by similar harsh-sounding instructions as they follow the various routes through the colliery, stopping and starting to their controller's commands. Yet, for all their conformity to the orders they are given and the uniform grimness of the life they share, each pony is shown to have an individual character. There are those that have breathing problems; there are those with sensitive noses; there are those that are always sensible and there are those that are often skittish. As a newcomer to pony leading and driving Jimmy is assigned to the quiet and reliable Frank.

A convincing and interesting account of just what ponies did is then given by the author as we share Jimmy's initiation into this new world. The technical details of how they hauled the different sized pit-props to the coal face or "inbye" are explained patiently to the young lad eager to come to terms with his new responsibility. There is a lot to learn and he sets his mind to do well. Yet, lingering in the background, through all of this part of the story, is the tragic knowledge, revealed on the first page of the book, that Jimmy is later going to be hauled up before the colliery manager, believing he has caused the death of one of the ponies. So, as the reader shares Jimmy's sense of achievement in mastering the new techniques of pony driving, there is also a general sense of foreboding and a more specific worry that an accident is just around the corner.

When the disaster happens the author makes it just enough of Jimmy's fault by placing him in a situation beyond his knowledge and experience to make us feel sorry for him, even though he has caused pain and suffering to the innocent animal. That fine balance between asking about what you don't know and the desire not to lose self-esteem and the confidence of your work-mates is brought out very well indeed. You are convinced that Jimmy should have known how to stop the overloaded runaway truck but you understand why the opportunity to gain the vital knowledge did not come along. It is the old problem of not knowing that you are out of depth until it is too late to do anything about it.

The harshness of the lesson that Jimmy has been taught is mitigated by the news that Frank has not been killed or put down as no longer useful. He is no longer fit for hauling materials down the pit and will be given a retirement above ground. Like Jimmy's father he has been "pensioned off" and the colliery manager, displaying a large amount of compassion and understanding about how Jimmy must be feeling, even suggests that the pony could join the old man on his allotment. The author has chosen to create happiness out of potential tragedy and made a valuable point about life in a dangerous working environment.

The Relics of War

The Secret of the Peel – 1948 (99) by Air Commodore Charlton is about the build-up to the Second World War and the events in Britain soon after the outbreak of that conflict. The story moves between Northumberland and Antigua in the West Indies and then, for the climax to the adventure, it returns to Northumberland again. As Peter Mawle lies on his sickbed in Hexham Hospital he begins to compose the account of what happened to him, his friend Tom Finch and Cy Lovelocks, the son of an American millionaire.

The story really begins when fourteen year old Peter is told by his father that he has "to take it on the chin" and realise that he will not be returning to Stagshaw College, a public school on the coast near to Holy Island. Bad financial advice and the resultant losses mean that the family will have to leave Allery Bank in Northumberland, the home of their ancestors, and live on a smaller scale on the island of Antigua where they still own some property. For Peter this means leaving behind his beloved pony, Spots, and abandoning his investigations of Mawlesike Peel. Although he is utterly downcast at this prospect, he realises that a shift to a warmer climate will be of real benefit to his ailing mother and makes up his mind to travel overseas without causing a fuss.

The author then introduces another strand of the plot which is to become of increasing importance. His father's cousin lives at Howlerhurst House nearby but the two families are not close because of Sir Geraint Mawle's involvement with the British Fascist Party. The old man is a leading member of the Buckle Union, formed for the purposes of peace and friendship with Hitler's Germany. Amongst other things this involves annual summer camps of young Germans at Howlerhurst. Already the avid reader of this sort of boys' adventure story can predict many of the events that are to come. There is a secret passage in Howlerhurst House and Peter believes that there are underground chambers at the old, remote Peel tower. Stir in some Germans on the brink of the war, drop in the fact that ghostly blue lights have been seen on the moor in the vicinity of the ruins, and you can see inevitably where this story is heading.

To this day the impact of the Second World War on the lonely hills and moors can still be traced in a fashion that surprises those who spend most of their lives in the big cities of the region. Littered across the landscape are large and small pieces of rusty metal that bear witness to the fate of many aeroplanes and their crews that flew across this region on dangerous operations. Quite a few of the casualties, alas, were young men on training flights whose equipment failed them or who made a fatal miscalculation. **The Camp at Auld-Man-Shiel** – 1948 (100), however, concerns itself with the mystery surrounding the fate of a German Heinkel which crashed on the slopes above Reedburn. The vital instruments were stripped out immediately but the carcass of the wreck remains embedded in the ground miles from the nearest habitation. Charlton brings out well the incongruity of such a machine in the middle of the rugged, unchanging yet constantly changeable natural scene. The landscape is wild but hypnotically attractive; the people who belong to the area have lived in the same way for centuries. The clannishness of the important families is still predominant in a way that is almost feudal with the same names appearing in the roles of squire, doctor, agent, tenant farmer and shepherd down the centuries. The son of the present landowner is called Robert Belham and he is home from his public school for the summer holidays. His best friend is Richard Spragge, the son of the local doctor. The two fifteen year old boys make up their minds that what they would most like to do is spend three weeks "living off the land" up on Monkside Fell with a camp at lonely Auld-Man-Shiel. With the use of very subtle detail L.E.O. Charlton shows how this apparent backwater of English life is feeling the austerity of a post-war Britain. Thus we learn that the Belham family find it very difficult to get "staff" in this changed world. An expedition to the hill-tops to gather "noops" or cloudberries is partly for fun and partly to supplement the meagre diet permitted by rationing. Stone walls knocked down by trainee tank drivers have not yet been rebuilt – there simply isn't the available manpower. However, it is startling to find, suddenly, in the middle of nowhere, a whole gang of German prisoners of war working to develop a plantation for the Forestry Commission.

Not all the old vestiges of countryside behaviour have been swept away by the war. The policemen still behave with excessive deference to Robert's father and the two boys on their so-called "self-sufficient" camping expedition have little qualms in deciding that Danny, a farm-labourer's son, would be useful to have in their camp as cook and general factotum. As they stroll around having fun "huntin" and "fishin" and exploring the crashed aircraft, Danny is back in camp doing the chores. The difference between the two classes is emphasised by the dialogue between the two public school boys which is heavily studded with expressions such as "getting a jawing" and "talking utter rot". Meanwhile Danny and the nearby farmers and shepherds are represented by phonetic variations on normal English words to suggest their accent. Every now and then a local expression or turn of phrase creeps into the discussion and convinces you that the author does have a genuine ear for language. Thus the bluntness of the expression "oe'r auld for the knife" to suggest that a man might not survive surgery gives the reader a feeling for the texture of the harsh life in some of the remote farms.

The adventure itself, involving gold coins, a drunken shepherd, a former member of the SAS, a local man who turned into a version of Lord Haw Haw, an escaped German, is surprising in its moderation. The boys face up to danger with courage but certainly know their limitations. They end up witnesses to the final acts of violence rather than participants. They do not solve the mystery by bravery or by intelligence but simply by being on the spot as events cascade to a conclusion around them.

Charlton moves from crashed aircraft to old gun emplacements as the centre for the mystery in *The Hut on Oh Me Edge* – 1949 (4B – see page 11 for 4A). Remember the two boys who got suspected of forgery in Section 1 of this book ? It's time to climb back on board their motorcycle.

Exonerated by a check with the local bank, they head out of Newcastle on to the Roman road and make their way to Bellingham. From then onwards they follow the valley of the North Tyne and find themselves for a while running alongside the railway which had an engine "of a style so antiquated that one had to rub one's eyes to believe it true". It's one of those branch lines that has now gone for ever, found only in old maps and works of local literature.

Much of the rest of the plot follows conventional lines with life in the hut proving perilous in the extreme. Hunting game supplements their diet and then hunting strange intruders leads to the climax of the book. As the boys stalk their prey the writer once again gives you a convincing feel for the lie of the land, the effects of the weather and the sounds of nature. It is strange to find that the criminal gang had their headquarters in Jesmond before they retreated to the remote countryside where one of their number served as a gunner during the war. It is even more peculiar to find that the mysterious stranger who sent the boys to Oh Me Edge (it is a real ridge !) in the first place wasn't on the trail of dangerous villains – he was merely worried about the setting up of a holiday camp in an area of natural beauty. Charlton's other book from this period is *The Mystery of Cowsole Wood* (66) which, after a short adventure on Brownsman in the Farne Islands, is set well outside this region.

The Reivers

A tale told through the night, by a storyteller proud of his craft and disdainful of his audience, is one that is sometimes simulated by authors who wish to give their readers a flavour of what it must have been like to be holed up round the fire on a long winter's evening. The story of ***Martin Farrell*** – 1994 (101) by Janni Howker is about the wild excesses of the border reivers, in particular the doings of the lawless clans of the Armstrongs, Elliotts, Nixons and Grahams. "Might is right" and "What I have, I hold" are just two of the selfish mottoes that apply in this story of internecine strife.

The nature of the narrative means that nothing is clear for a long time and, when it becomes clear, the horror of understanding is worse than the earlier doubt that precedes it. There's nothing at all romantic in this story of the thefts, rapes and murders that are brutally put in front of his audience by a storyteller who runs the whole gamut of attitudes from sneering sarcasm and brutal insult to wistful regret.

The story itself begins at the wedding of young Will Armstrong, the last remaining son of the old clan chief, to Anne Elliott. A word out of place brings about the death of the man whom fourteen year old Martin Farrell had known as his father. The inoffensive man was killed and his entrails eaten by a black pig. Martin himself is eventually taken to the house of the Grahams by a travelling Galloway fiddler. There he learns that the widow of the Graham chieftain is his own grandmother. Eventually the rest of the appalling tale comes out. The Grahams and the Armstrongs are deadly enemies, maintaining a blood feud that stretches back into remote history. The Armstrongs generally have the upper hand but, when caught in the act of robbery one day, the son of the chief Armstrong is hanged by the Grahams stringing his own belt round his neck. Old Armstrong takes his revenge by raping the daughter of the Graham chieftain. The product of this violent union is Martin. To his horror he realises that his blood is the blood of both warring families. His inheritance seems to be to die hated by both families and their retainers because he now knows the truth.

The only quiet notes in the whole story are brought out by the new bride, Anne Armstrong, hating every day the way the husband in her bed chamber who can be so loving, is transformed when he leaves her to be with his father, the evil Old Armstrong.

Towards the end of the story Martin spends a night on the hillside confronting temptation which arrives in the form of ghosts and spirits. In the inevitable blood-letting the next day when both clans catch up with him, Martin takes the role of witness rather than protagonist, and the most evil men on either side of the feud, including his horrific beast of a father, Old Armstrong, are killed. Young Will Armstrong is ready to recognise Martin as his brother and the book ends with the birth of the first child of Will and Anne in a time of peace.

It would be of little use to try to trace the places mentioned in the book. It is a challenging read for anyone, whether young or old, for the brutality and, surprisingly, also the tenderness, have to be disentangled from the jerky, disconnected narrative, jumbled descriptions and the consistently hectoring delivery of the wild storyteller. It is certainly a counterblast to all those who think that the story of the reivers is a wild and romantic one.

A Haunted Tale

Three significant features in the Northumberland countryside stand at the centre of the fantasy tale, ***The House with No Windows*** – 1977 (102), by Allan Jermieson set in a lonely hollow. The hills of Northumberland and their wild but attractive remoteness make the most important contribution to the tale. The massive edifice of the Roman Wall snakes across them and introduces the idea of man's work into this untamed environment. Last, but not least, there is the new dam (perhaps based on the idea of Kielder) which is about to spread the tentacles of its power lines and pylons as it carries electricity to the south. That the story is set in the countryside near the wall is certain but the details are kept fictitious and place names have been altered (Hexington and Nesterton are just two that the author supplies) or suppressed. In the midst of this real but vague terrain Allan Jermieson gives a close evocation of his own particular chosen imagined landscape – the eerie but beautiful Witchstone Hollow.

His chief protagonist is a thirteen year old girl, called Donna Karen, who has come to live in a small cottage in the deserted landscape for a year with her father and her mother. From the very first day the young girl is struck by a powerful feeling about the past in this place which she has already partially glimpsed in a painting presented to her mother by a mysterious stranger. Three buildings now become the core of her new life. At first sight the most striking of these is the mansion mentioned in the title, the house of a self-made business magnate called Brinker, an ugly building of yellow sandstone, which was never completed when its owner was physically deformed and mentally scarred in an accident in one of his mills. The second building is the old observatory up on the ridge, the place where Brinker finally ended his life by hanging himself from one its rails. More reassuring than either of these is the cottage where she lives, built in the shape of a Viking long-house and remarkably comforting in the way it is divided into joint occupation for the people and the horses.

So much for the present and the near past (Brinker lived in the 19th century) – for it is with the more distant past and the stuff of myth and legend that Donna Karen finds herself suddenly connecting by a series of alarming visions. Extracts from Northumbrian legends, nationally known folklore and unexplained happenings in history are the basis for the series of dramas that the author conjures up. Did King Arthur really find his last resting place under these hills and does he sleep still ready to be roused when England needs him ? Do the circles of standing stones still to be found in the remote places of Northumberland and other English counties retain the powers they were once believed to have in the days when they were the centres of pagan rituals ? Do the remnants of the lost legions of Rome wander the mists of time, revealing themselves every now and then to those chosen for their particular sensibilities – like Donna Karen ? These are representative of the sorts of themes that the author develops as we learn more and more about the lonely and frightening hollow.

The most powerful and relevant theme of all is that man should learn to work with nature and the old ways and not in defiance of it. Thus Brinker, who smashed the sacred stones of the circle and built his house without windows on the top, is crushed in the mill and the road to his mansion is buried in a devastating landslip. Donna Karen finds that the centre stone still remains in the lip of a well and that it seems to be the channel through which both power and knowledge might flow. In the observatory, which Brinker had built on the crest of the ridge, she finds that he has tapped into an underground spring that produces the hydraulic power to rotate its turret as he followed the stars through the night sky. However, she also sees the bend in the metal bar where the rope that choked away his life was attached. As she tries to come to terms with these visions and take some form of decisive action she has two "ghostly" companions. One is the mysterious Peter the painter (who is also Pertinax, the lost Roman commander) and the second is the other-worldly black horse called Erondore. He is made both a real horse of the present and a steed whom Peter has ridden in the past. Donna Karen continually finds herself facing the dangers and rising to the challenges that are thrown in front of her. She is made to realise that she has access to power that is both creative and destructive. Passive knowledge has to be replaced by a desire to tackle evil. A particularly effective passage in the book is the battle with fire against the group of trees which seem to have inherited all the seductive power of the witches after whom the hollow is named.

Though it is acknowledged that the dam has to be built, for progress cannot be stopped, the author uses the metaphor of "painting it brown" to suggest that it could be developed in harmony with the landscape it will occupy. Instead, each day Donna Karen sees only the relentless march of the pylons destroying the countryside, with the same brutal disregard that Brinker had shown when he smashed the stone circle. A series of dreams and visions tell her that she is the one who must find the underground power and release it to bring this desecration to an end.

In a story like this where the author makes his own rules about the relative powers of natural magic and the interconnected nature of history and landscape, the reader can sometimes end up either confused or feeling cheated. However, it is to the credit of Allan Jermieson that he keeps his vision consistent and that there are many passages of truly exciting writing.

The Adventures Completed

It is time now to pick up the adventures of the four young teenagers in **The Witch of Redesdale** (9B – see page 12 for 9A) who set off from Central Station by bike in our first section about Newcastle.

Later, as they follow the Newcastle to Jedburgh road to the Catcleugh Reservoir, the details of the Border Ballads are related to the hills and heather that surround them by the romantic Gill who has learned so many lines of poetry by heart. As we travel back 50 years to live in the author's world of the four characters, so they hark back further to the time when Scots and English carried on an unceasing, bloody war with many feuds and battles. The continuity of Northumbrian history is ironically underlined by the notices erected by the Ministry of Defence that tell them and us that these lands are still used and are still "VERY DANGEROUS".

The biggest risk that Winifred Finlay takes is with her creation of Auld Madge who is the eponymous "Witch of Redesdale". Her appearance, with her long greasy locks of hair and a face yellowed by dirt, is quite shocking and she seems to have all the sinister malevolence of a creature that has strayed into the story from "Macbeth". The fact that Madge has perversely called her two cats Graymalkin and Blackmalkin does little to discourage the village folk of Redeshaugh from believing that she is a force for evil that both frightens them and drives them to acts of violence. In contrast the four children set about tackling the squalor in which the old woman lives, meeting her provocative jibes with a kind of cheeky defiance that Madge begins to relish. There is certainly a mystery to be solved and villains to overcome, and the story eventually wends its way back to the bottle of quack medicine that was purchased in the first chapter. However, it is not really the plot that holds your attention but the fascinating eerie nature of certain scenes, like the finding of the injured cat in the fairy-tale dark wood or the gentle comedy of Brian's attempt to milk a reluctant goat.

There is a moment in Arthur Ransome's "Swallowdale" where the Swallows and the Amazons climb the mountain that has become for them Kanchenjunga. As they explore the cairn at the top they uncover a box which reveals to Nancy and Peggy that their mother and father and uncle had climbed the same hill some twenty-five years before, only for them they were conquering the Matterhorn. All at once their stolen adventures, which have seemed at times rather risky and selfish, become vindicated in a solemn moment of identity with their dead father, their now rather down-trodden mother and their somewhat irascible but kindly uncle. It is a similar feeling of connection with the past and those who have gone before that Winifred Finlay tries to explore in *Mystery in the Middle Marches* – 1964 (27B – see page 26 for 27A). Just what happened to Ethelinda March, a distant ancestor of twins Simon and Jane, is the strong thread that binds together this story of the wild places of north Northumberland and the Scottish border during the depths of winter and the coming of spring. All the typical Winifred Finlay ingredients now begin to merge into another attractive, exciting and ultimately quite moving adventure. To unravel the details would spoil the grip of the mystery but real places are again used skilfully and evocatively. At the little village school the smaller children dream of the North Sea being frozen, and of climbing on to the Tyne at Hexham and skating down to the mouth of the big river, and then on until they reach Norway.

Later, as the story leaps to remote Northumberland, we are invited to puzzle at the actions of the woman who was prepared to walk "widdershins" around the lonely Kielder Stone and to feel the effects of a thunderstorm on an abandoned farmhouse. Yet again a young boy, originally both anti-girls and against all non-Scots, is brought round to considering that Jane is somehow different and worthy of his respect. Even Ursula, the rebellious and permanently depressed eighteen year old daughter of the local vicar, discovers something within herself that she hadn't suspected was there. The solution to the Ethelinda puzzle proves even more surprising than the details had suggested and the twins realise that the tentacles of the past still have a surprising capacity to spring out and claim them.

And now let us return to the adventure that began with the unexpected lift from the Haymarket Bus Station. *Storm Over Cheviot* – 1955 (12B – see page 15 for 12A), in a way, is the most remarkable of Winifred Finlay's Northumberland books. It is only in the last thirty pages that you realise that she has left behind the usual tales of boys and girls and turned her narrative into a tale of redemption. On this occasion the capacity she has shown for allowing her readers to learn gradually about the important characters is made subject to a period of tremendous acceleration.

For once Winifred Finlay reverses the normal state of affairs and makes young Jo Kerr, the little girl who lives in the remote house with her grandfather, into the implacable enemy of the opposite sex. In particular she is antagonistic to Richard, though she considers herself the enemy to all Nortons because of ancient tribal conflicts. Richard's imaginary world is curtailed by the no-nonsense attitudes of his elder brother and his uncle. Jo suffers from no such restraint for her grandfather is a remote man, totally bound up in his studies of Celtic stone circles and his ideas about Bronze Age education. When Richard, Paul and Bill are joined by Mrs. Norton and her grown-up daughter, Judith, who have come to stay for a while in a remote cottage in the College Valley, they are all alarmed and disturbed by the way in which the little girl disappears into the wild countryside for days on end. Mrs. Norton rightly diagnoses that, tough and independent as she might seem, little Jo is missing her mother who is abroad in Kenya. When the blizzard descends on the valley and the little girl disappears once more a search is mounted where Richard gets himself dangerously side-tracked but finds Jo. Their difference forgotten, they work together to make their way to safety.

However, the real bite of the story is yet to come. Jo's forays into the lonely hillside were to take food to Flash Baker, whose latest venture into crime came badly unstuck and who is now on the run. The little girl's imagination has turned him into a border raider that she must protect at all costs. How Flash is both rescued and captured is recounted with exciting vividness – his selfish cowardice being emphasised by many small but telling incidents. As the blizzard intensifies the Nortons realise that they are all trapped together with a young criminal and a little girl who is now dangerously ill. Until the weather moderates there is no way out and no way in for the doctor who is badly needed.

It is at this point that Mrs. Norton has a series of interviews with the thoroughly cowed Flash Baker. She learns of how the young spiv had avoided National Service and boasted of this fact to Richard and Paul. It is then that she reveals how they must have felt as he told this tale. Their father, her husband, had been a fighter pilot and had given his life so that people like Flash could be free to live how they wanted. Their uncle, her brother Bill, had also listened to Flash's tales of outwitting the law and dodging his duty. Bill had been in the navy, risking his life and passing through many awful but untold experiences only to see what he had fought for being abused. Little Jo, however deluded she may have been about her motives, had set out into the snowstorm, to keep faith with Flash, because she believed it was her duty. Now she is likely to pay the ultimate price for that misguided loyalty. This catalogue of home truths is then set against the morally bankrupt nature of Flash's upbringing to devastating effect.

The only way out for the trapped people is through the tremendous snow-drifts; the only way out for the penitent Flash is through a stupendous effort of atonement, where his finely honed driving skills are for once used to good effect. It is the parable of the lost sheep taken a stage further.

Chillingham

It is sometimes forgotten just what extreme contrasts lie between the different parts of this north-eastern region of the country. It can rightly be said that there are "regions within regions". This contrast is well-exemplified by Frederick Grice's book ***The Courage of Andy Robson*** – 1969 (103) which takes a boy from a small mining village (here called Sleetburn) on the Durham coalfield and drops him into the middle of the Northumberland countryside. In several other books Grice and other authors like Richard Armstrong have shown us the countryside that surrounds the workings of industry. However, when Andy boards the train in Durham station and then alights at Lilburn it is as though he has travelled to a whole new world. The railway line that takes him there is a symbol of the modern, industrialised environment from which he has come; the pony and trap in which he is driven by his uncle through the heart of the fields and the forests represents an older, quieter and slower way of life.

For Andy everything is different and he notes especially the different accent of his uncle and the different smells in the air. Above all there is the apparent silence. The word "apparent" is used advisedly for later Andy gradually attunes himself to the songs of the birds and the bleating of the sheep. A near-tragic family accident in the pit has brought him to his country relations and, for a while, he feels like he has been thrust into a world which he cannot learn to accept. In particular the ways of the country boys seem to him to be extraordinary. He has to learn a whole new set of rules and of values. The boys in Sleetburn fight with their fists but in Lilburn they wrestle. The boys in the village all know how to knit and for Andy this was an occupation only for women. He has been used to singing out lustily in the Methodist chapel but in the local Lilburn church he is seen as an oddity and is browbeaten into silence by the disapproving words of the local squire, Lord Hetherington. Inevitably the "foreign" nature of this strange land brings on a bout of homesickness.

However, Grice's book is not just about Andy's struggle to come to terms with his new destiny, and very soon the author begins to talk about the one remarkable feature that makes Lilburn stand out not just from all of Northumberland but from the rest of the world. This is the famous herd of wild white cattle and the giant enclosure in which they are kept. This fictionalised version of the real Chillingham herd, one of the marvels of present-day Northumberland, becomes very important to Andy, and not just because his uncle is the park ranger responsible for their care. When the story of the book unfolds it becomes clear that Andy's future is tied up with the survival of these unique animals. It is also apparent that events in his life are made to parallel significant happenings in the life-cycle of the cattle. Thus when a calf is born there is a ritualistic inspection of the new arrival by the key members of the rest of the herd, mirroring closely Andy's gradual acceptance into the close community of Lilburn. More importantly, the herd has a king bull who leads the others and makes all the vital decisions. From time to time his authority is challenged by young bucks who seek to overturn him and often die in the fight. By the end of the book Andy has learned the skill of wrestling and defeated the bully, Billy Craggs, who has led the tribe of boys in the village for too long. Grice extends the implied comparison a stage further by having Lord Hetherington, who has neglected and even hunted the unique animals for the amusement of his ignorant guests, yield the power of ownership and care to his more caring and intelligent son.

The key episode in which Andy proves he has the "courage" that is mentioned in the title of the book arises out of the natural cycle of the seasons and is part of a tremendous description of a countryside in the icy grip of a seemingly never-ending winter. Suddenly the survival of the herd depends upon him and Grice leads us carefully through the steps that lead the animals to the brink of extinction. His achievement is that the search for the dead and the living when the snows have finally retreated becomes of a personal concern to the reader as well as Andy and his uncle.

Though he mostly presents us with a picture of kind, good-natured and hard-working people, Grice introduces enough malcontents and petty bullies and enough bleakness and hardship to convince us that life in the countryside in the 19th century was not idyllic. It comes as a surprise that those working down the pit earned a better wage and indeed that sometimes they enjoyed better living conditions. When Andy, his enforced holiday over, finds himself back in his Durham pit-village, he realises that there is something missing. He may actually be better off in terms of the economics of life but the challenge of looking after the Lilburn cattle and preserving them for the future is now irresistible. He has earned the right to do so and when the call comes from the north he has no hesitation in persuading his family that he must answer it. Did Andy succeed in this new world? All we know is that the old Northumberland railway line to Wooler is gone but the white cattle of Lilburn (or rather Chillingham) are still with us.

The Scout Story
The only example of this is *The Secret of Rumbling Churn* by John Sweet – 1953 (104).

For the purpose of creating a Scout camp story the author invented the ideal environment. The boys in Cuckoo Patrol camp on an island in the middle of a river, upstream of which there is an underground cave. The nearest village is Westbrae – somewhere in north Northumberland. Nearby is the dark bulk of Black Rigg with the red flag of danger fluttering from its heather-clad summit warning of imminent explosions in the quarry. The only other clue to the location of this story comes in Chapter XII when two of the Scouts travel in a friend's car on a trip to Hexham. The road heads south for a journey of at least an hour, travelling at forty-five miles per hour on a road which is like a switchback. The book was written in 1953 and so you can see the challenge of making the calculations and pinning this story to an exact place.

The plot concerns a secret from the past and a modern day robbery. Somehow they are both linked to the noise that issues from a particular cave when the rain falls and the river rises. Some of the clues to the secret are found on the aforementioned visit that is paid to Hexham on market day when the Scouts go through the old records in the local library. Incidentally the Commander (the Scouts' friend and driver of the car) easily found "a convenient parking place in one of the leafy by-roads near the abbey". Later the boys enjoy a slap-up meal of steak pie in a local hotel (unfortunately unnamed).

The book builds to a satisfying climax with the character conflicts between the scouts being resolved, with the psychological damage to their friend being repaired and an exciting chase of a villain armed with dynamite.

The End of the Journeys

In a county as large as Northumberland the potential for exciting and arduous journeys is obvious. Several writers have used this "largeness" together with extremes of weather in order to drive their books to very effective peaks of excitement. It is inevitable that we must mention once again several stories by Lorna Hill.

Dress Rehearsal – 1959 (29) describes in detail the journey by Nona Browning and Vicki Scott from Keswick to Newcastle. Their method of travel is a mixture of hitch-hiking and walking. The added excitement is gained from the fact that Nona is on the run from the obnoxious household where she has been placed in service by one of the governors of the Newcastle children's home. Vicki, the spoiled only child of her family, has seen that Nona's vocation is to be a ballet dancer. However, temporarily short of ready money, the only way to get to Newcastle and to substitute Nona into the dress rehearsal of the title is to travel secretly. The stretch of the journey from Carlisle to Newcastle is broken by a night spent in the caretaker's hut at Housesteads Roman fort. The series of "lifts" along the Military Road and then the A69 provides a fascinating variety to the storyline. In both *Masquerade at the Wells* and ***Jane Leaves the Wells*** (3) we are reminded that Housesteads was the destination for the pony ride of young Jane when she rescued the sheep and demonstrated to herself for the first time that she is not lacking in courage and determination. A much more arduous ride was made by Veronica, Sebastian and Caroline in the second of the "Wells" series, entitled ***Veronica at the Wells*** – 1951 (105). In late December the three set out on their ponies from their home near Bellingham to ride beyond the Coquet to a little farm called Broomyhough. They cross the A68 above Alwinton and finally reach their destination. But winter days are short and as they begin the long trek home the snow starts to fall thick and fast. The delicate Veronica begins to feel exhaustion seeping over her as she becomes mesmerised by the black strips of road in between the drifts of snow as her pony slowly ploughs onwards. Only drastic action by Sebastian can save her from falling into the treacherous final sleep.

Another young Lorna Hill hero makes a vital contribution in the story entitled ***Dancing Peel*** – 1954 (106). The peel in question is at Mintlaw not too far from Otterburn. It's a remote place indeed but becomes even more so after a period of torrential rain which causes floods and washes away most of the local bridges. Poor Annette, the heroine, is totally distressed for she had hoped to travel into Newcastle that day in order to take her vital ballet examination. She believes that on her success in this series of tests depends all her future. Angus tries to get her to the Bellingham bus by offering her a place in front of him on the saddle of his horse. When they get to the streams he will dismount and wade across, leading her safely behind him. As they come to the deepest stream, the Tarret Burn, Annette suddenly confesses that it was she who had played a spiteful trick on him on the day before. Once again Angus rises to the occasion – in this kind of story he could hardly do otherwise.

When the man whom you have always thought of as your father tells you that he isn't then it is bound to produce a total dislocation in your way of thinking. To discover on top of this that you have been sired by a Norman, one of the hated master race who have taken over England, only adds to your confusion. In ***Knights of the Sacred Blade*** – 1989 (44) by Julian Atterton, this is the fate which befalls Simon who suddenly realises that he is Simon de Falaise, the son of itinerant adventurer, Sir Jordan.

Simon's quiet life in Guisborough is over for, though he loves his home, he knows that he wants to start to see the world. At first it seems his journeys round the north of

England and over the border into Scotland are destined to be mere wanderings without purpose. Sir Jordan is a landless knight, seeking constantly territory to hold on behalf of a more senior member of the Norman hierarchy. Very soon, however, Simon and his new friend, Aimeric the scholar, stumble on to an ancient mystery which could lead them to the sacred blade of the old Saxon kings. There are riddles to be solved and dangerous journeys to be made. Worst of all, perhaps, is the knowledge that others are pursuing the same quest and that they are ruthless men who will stop at nothing to gain this powerful symbol.

Gradually, just like young Simon, the reader is able to piece together the British political situation in 1135. The shrewd and ruthless King Henry I of England has died leaving no legitimate son to follow him and the inevitable war breaks out to decide the succession. On one side is Stephen of Blois (Henry's nephew) and on the other, the Empress Matilda (Henry's daughter). This is the ideal opportunity for the Scottish king to strike against Stephen's northern strongholds whilst the new English king is busy subduing his subjects in the south. It is to the credit of Julian Atterton that he manages to give brief and convincing pictures of both monarchs. In particular his depiction of King David is intriguing in the way that he brings out the differing sides of the man by referring to the qualities he has inherited from his warlike father and his saint-like mother. Archbishop Thurstan who rallies the English (both Norman and Saxon) before the Battle of the Standard (near Northallerton) is also portrayed in some depth.

Mostly, however, this a story about constant journeying and more places in the North are mentioned in this book than any of the other children's stories set in the North-East. Much of the later part of the story is concerned with the siege of the border stronghold of Carham where Simon's father holds out against the Scots long after Norham and Bamburgh have been forced to surrender.

This little village on the border with Scotland brings us back to our 1314 story of **Ransom for a Knight** (23B – see page 22 for 23A) by Barbara Leonie Picard. We left young Alys and Hugh finally leaving Newcastle after a three week delay because of illness. Between Morpeth and Alnwick they are forced to pass through a village where the plague has broken out. All riders on the road are now to be treated with suspicion and they have to keep plunging off into the woods and the moorland. Eventually, of course, they end up lost.

Barbara Leonie Picard chooses to place the peak of their ordeal, the worst point of their journey, on a lonely farm in the north of Northumberland. Snow is falling and Christmas is approaching and Alys has become dangerously ill. The farmer's wife is hostile and even shelter in an outhouse is grudgingly given by the farmer himself. By Christmas Day Alys is on the brink of death and Hugh has no food to give to her. There then follows a visit to a repulsive looking and harsh-speaking wise-woman or witch. The whole of this episode on the lonely farm is both extremely harrowing and marvellously touching. The author shows us both the best and worst of the northern character in the differing attitudes of the people on the farm towards the children and the witch.

When Alys is just well enough to travel they are forced to back-track towards Hulne Priory and later to Alnwick where they are reduced once again to begging. Unfortunately their troubles are very far from being over, for they fall in with a bunch of thieves and get caught up in a hue and cry that sees them make their escape to Alnmouth. From there they move north again past Dunstanburgh Castle and Newton and so to Berwick. At his point they move out of our region but we must follow the author a little further.

The essence of the book so far has been following how Alys and Hugh get on both with each other and with the people they have met on their journey. The narrative has been crammed with details of medieval life including many vivid glimpses of Northumbria. A considered review would reveal that they have met cruelty and kindness in equal measure. It is a harsh world but there are some good people in it. Though they come from opposite ends of the social framework, they have also discovered aspects of their character that have bound them together. The servant is as good as his mistress but the girl is as brave and resolute as the boy.

The surprise is that when they cross the border the world doesn't change. In spite of all their fears Scotland is neither populated by savages nor saints. The kindness and honesty of ordinary people surprises them and the two children eventually come across a Scots farmer and his family who help them on their way and ensure that the quest is successful.

The journey of this book about children's stories began at Central Station. I hope you will agree that it is appropriate that we finish at the Scottish border with this story of hope revived and faith renewed.

Remember what we said at the beginning. If you know of any children's story (not folk-tale or legend, nor a story which has the childhood of a character but which was clearly written with adults in mind) that is set in Newcastle, North Tyneside or Northumberland, than please contact me via the publishers of this book.

Post Script – A Few More Miles, A Few More Books

MY prediction about more books turning up has already been fulfilled. It is not really surprising to come across a new book by David Almond. There is just time to tell you that **The Fire Eaters** (August 2003) has scenes set on Newcastle Quayside and in a small (fictional) resort on the Northumberland coast. This is now this region's newest children's book – until the next one.

Much more unexpected was my discovery of the region's oldest children's book **Wildcat Tower** by G. Christopher Davies which was first published in 1876. It could happily be fitted into any of the stages of our journey for, like this modest volume, it begins on Central Station, contains a description of a journey down the Tyne to Tynemouth, devotes a section to Bamburgh Castle, the Chillingham cattle and a trip to the Farnes; there is also an exploration of the Roman Wall and a paddle in a coracle on Crag Lough. In fact it truly lives up to its sub-title: **Adventures of Four Boys in Pursuit of Sport and Natural History in the North Countrie.** At 322 pages and with up to 50 illustrations it is also probably the region's longest children's book.

By sheer accident I discovered that **Grace** by the award-winning author Jill Paton Walsh was not a biography of Grace Darling but a fictionalised account for young adults of the effect of fame on this heroine of the Longstone. In contrast **The Lost Legionary** (1995) by Mick Gowar is a book in the Sparks series for very young readers and recounts the experiences of young Gaius in his father's army camp near Housesteads. Thinking of the Romans again stirred my memory for Rosemary Sutcliff's adventures and I should like to add to the list **The Silver Branch** which has its own brief but exciting Roman Wall episode.

Scanning through booksellers' lists on the internet brought to my attention a book called **Explorers on the Wall** (1939) by Garry Hogg. This is a family story with adventures taking place all along the Wall and detailed illustrations and plans intended to appeal (as the dust-jacket claims) to "Map Minded" readers of any age. Even more than **Wildcat Tower** Garry Hogg's book is a real relic of the past, with much of the adventure relying upon the character of an extraordinarily long-suffering uncle and a plot based around the escape and dangerous antics of a weird-looking lunatic. They don't write them like that any more.

Even as I write this last sentence and think about a different journey into County Durham or to the Lake District I am aware that there are other northern books out there. Someone has just told me that Terry Deary has several other stories, set back in the past, which begin in a hall near Newcastle . . .